MW00917395

Journey to the
Heart of Darkness

Remembering Congo's Forgotten

Trésor Yenyi

iUniverse, Inc.
New York Bloomington

Journey to the Heart of Darkness
Remembering Congo's Forgotten

iUniverse books may be ordered through booksellers or by contacting:

iUniverse
1663 Liberty Drive
Bloomington, IN 47403
www.iuniverse.com
1-800-Authors (1-800-288-4677)

ISBN: 978-1-4502-5816-6 (pbk)
ISBN: 978-1-4502-5814-2 (cloth)
ISBN: 978-1-4502-5815-9 (ebk)

Printed in the United States of America

iUniverse rev. date: 10/5/10

"Soli Deo Gloria"

I want to say thank you to:

My parents Victor and Pauline Yenyi for your love and support; thank you for teaching me to love and be compassionate toward others. Thanks for all the sacrifices you made to raise us.

To my sisters Rose, Joelle, Denise, and to my brothers Pierre and Deo. Thanks for being part of this dream and working so hard in helping it become a reality.

To Christian Kunkadi, thanks for always being there for me and standing by me no matter what challenge the world brings.

To Vernon and Lucille, thanks for treating me like your own son for all these years.

To Amanda Adkins, Chad Harrington, Erica Humphrey, Glendola Flake, John Hunter, Karl Mitchell, Kaylene Williamson and Meredith Moser. Thank you for making this possible.

Catherine Thorpe, thank you for taking me through the healing timeline.

This book is really a gift from Judie Kakac. Judie is a lady who has a special place in my heart. She is not Congolese, has never been to Africa. But Judie loved me and adopted me as her son and I have adopted her as my fourth mother. I am very fortunate to have mothers from all over the world. Judie prepared some very special envelopes for each day of my trip. She included little papers with scriptures on them as well as candies. She also gave me the journals that became the basis for this book.

Thanks Judie, you are amazing!

This book is dedicated to all the innocent victims of the war in the Democratic Republic of Congo.

CONTENTS

Part IV: From Doubt to a Place of Abundance 79

PSALM 10

1 [a]Why, O LORD, do you stand far off?
  Why do you hide yourself in times of trouble?
2 In his arrogance the wicked man hunts down the weak,
  who are caught in the schemes he devises.
3 He boasts of the cravings of his heart;
  he blesses the greedy and reviles the LORD.
4 In his pride the wicked does not seek him;
  in all his thoughts there is no room for God.
5 His ways are always prosperous;
  he is haughty and your laws are far from him;
  he sneers at all his enemies.
6 He says to himself, "Nothing will shake me;
  I'll always be happy and never have trouble."
7 His mouth is full of curses and lies and threats;
  trouble and evil are under his tongue.
8 He lies in wait near the villages;
  from ambush he murders the innocent,
  watching in secret for his victims.
9 He lies in wait like a lion in cover;
  he lies in wait to catch the helpless;
  he catches the helpless and drags them off in his net.
10 His victims are crushed, they collapse;
  they fall under his strength.
11 He says to himself, "God has forgotten;
  he covers his face and never sees."
12 Arise, LORD! Lift up your hand, O God.
  Do not forget the helpless.
13 Why does the wicked man revile God?
  Why does he say to himself,
  "He won't call me to account"?
14 But you, O God, do see trouble and grief;
  you consider it to take it in hand.
  The victim commits himself to you;
  you are the helper of the fatherless.
15 Break the arm of the wicked and evil man;
  call him to account for his wickedness
  that would not be found out.
16 The LORD is King for ever and ever;
  the nations will perish from his land.
17 You hear, O LORD, the desire of the afflicted;
  you encourage them, and you listen to their cry,
18 defending the fatherless and the oppressed,
  in order that man, who is of the earth, may terrify no more.

FORWARD

In 1979, a hungry little boy would interrupt an ordinary man named Larry Jones - the request; a simple nickel to buy food. It wasn't so simple a nickel that would provide food to a child who hadn't eaten in days - and it wasn't so simple an interruption in the life of a man who, as a result of a passion to help children, would embark on a journey to build one of the largest humanitarian organizations in history.

We all have them; interruptions. On average, you can expect one every 8 minutes of every hour of every day. Over 20,000 pauses in a year - yet they're not all the same. Some matter so great that they make a difference. Some in fact, are moments in time when, to the watchful and educated eye, everything in your world can change.

They are what some call "divine appointments" with destiny. They are the times in our life where we come face-to-face with what can only be described as a supernatural intersection. A moment when (to the watchful and aware), we are presented with an opportunity to make a decision to heed a "call" to something that is bigger than us. A break in the morning, the day or the night, when our life begins to make sense and we transform from just ordinary to the incredible. For many, these breaks in the norm are profound. For most who don't know how to interpret them

- they're just another fascinating "bleep" on the radar of our life; perhaps moving, emotional moments that are factored as nothing more than intriguing or coincidental. For those of us who are paying attention, like you are right now...they set the stage for an incredible journey of change.

Flip through the pages of the Bible and you will observe a book of just such moments in time. Interruptions that mattered. Observe that a man was let down through a hole in a roof, and an interruption of Jesus would result in healing. An interruption of the man called Christ while teaching, led to the remarkable feeding of 5,000 with just a few loaves of bread and fish.

God is seeking to "interrupt" your life and reveal to you a journey that will set everything in your world, all of your planets of purpose in orbit. Sometimes, he will lead us down a path, to a job, into the life of someone or someone into our life - and the pause in time we so loosely label an "interruption" actually changes everything. And to those attuned to recognize it and who have the understanding to interpret, it is the combustible element that activates the great love of God, he is trying so desperately to show.

Mine came under the heat of a 108 degree burning sun, surrounded by hundreds of small children who had never seen a television camera or cell phone. In the heart of a village that literally looked like the land time forgot, my journey to the Congo led me into the deepest, hottest, most remote and desperate part of Africa, and an interruption that would set the stage for the greatest change in my world and a pursuit to understand what small steps that I could take to do my part to help the innocent in a hurting world. In a country that is full of beautiful waters and majestic rainforests, the Congo is also home to a war that has raged long. As warring militia groups inflict suffering that the media nor this book can adequately capture, the lives of over four million men, women and children have been lost, leaving the country in poverty, wrought with disease and victim to some of the most incredible heinous acts that could befall the innocent. But the Congo also revealed to me truths about the strength, focus and hard-wired survival instinct woven into the fabric of the human condition. In my willingness to take the time to watch, to listen and to learn, a little crippled boy who stopped the cameras asking to show me game with rocks and twigs, marked an interruption that changed my world, and an intersection of our worlds, which has led him walking today.

This is not a textbook chronicling the death and suffering of a people you do not know. It is a snapshot of the aftermath of one of the deadliest ongoing wars since Hitler marched across Europe, and how such an interruption of a revealing truth found in the heart of a darkness, might transform your thinking, shape your world and provide you with the opportunity to make a difference.

As you crack the cover of this book and flip through its pages, you are bringing "pause" into your world to hear something different. The sound is the voice of a small child, the plea of the hopeless; the desperate pitch of the plight of the innocent that shatters reasoning and that disrupts our complacency. The rat-a-tat-tat of innocent hearts is calling out for someone to intersect their broken world, and nothing that I have ever read profiles the hidden truth of such a people, and an opportunity to make a difference, than the book you now hold in your hands right now.

Your journey begins in Chapter one on page one. The choice to hear is yours. The interruption was made and the stage is set for your discovery of a world you knew nothing about, that will shed a light into darkness that before today, you might never have known or ever had the chance to see. This interruption is worth it. As you discover the reality that exists here, your paradigm about your place in the world will shift and your mind will change related to how great and valuable a simple step, a helping hand or a prayer can be in the life of the world's hurting people. Inked on paper within these pages, is the beating heart of a boy who would know this country, who would survive it, and who became a man willing to tell a story to those who would choose to listen.

Prepare to be interrupted. This book will intersect you and motivate you to make a mark in the life of another that cannot be erased.

Damon S. Davis,
CEO of Legacy Group Global

PROLOGUE

When I was a child, occasionally my father would tell us stories. We sat down around him as we listened carefully to the tales of his childhood. My mother was also a good story teller. She told us stories of the wars she experienced as a child in Kisangani. My mother narrated so vividly that we felt transported to the moment the rebels were attacking Kisangani. From my parents, I learned to love telling stories, especially those that inspire people to take action against the injustice in the world. I was born in Eastern Congo in 1983 at the peak of Mobutu's reign. I was "privileged" to witness history in the making. I saw the country fall into chaos. I have been an eyewitness to looting, war and corruption. I saw Congo glide into its grave.

It was during these years I developed a passion for the weak and the oppressed. As the years went by, I felt an increasing need to somehow bring a change. I was dissatisfied with the way we lived in Congo. I wanted to bring hope to the lives of my countrymen. I was one of the few children lucky enough to go to school in my own neighborhood, so I always felt I was carrying a burden for those who could not go to school. Even though I barely associated with them, they still had a special part in my life.

The desire to write a book started springing up inside of me during my teenage years, when I developed a love for writing. I often read my father's law books even though they were complicated. At that time, I also learned to love ancient writings, I was amazed by these great storytellers and I knew someday I would write a book. I always wanted to write something meaningful; something that would contribute in telling stories that the world needed to hear.

I moved to the United States when I was twenty-one. Once I moved, the desire to write this book became more prominent, as my passion for the poor and oppressed grew on the campus of Ozark Christian College in Joplin, Missouri. No longer would I be compassionate merely in words, but I was going to show compassion with my deeds. This journey led to the creation of Mwangaza Congo International, a nonprofit organization that works with war victims. This prompted a few trips back to my homeland in search of a cure for the cancer that Congo suffers. Having grown up in the Congo and then having been exposed to American culture, I had a unique way of viewing the situation in the Congo. Having experienced peace in America, I longed for the troubled land of my ancestors to find peace again.

While I was actually living in the Congo, I did not realize how much the country had fallen into the pit of a tragedy. When I came to Joplin, the easy access to information helped me realize the depth of what was going on, in every corner of my homeland. Statistics, numbers, and news reports, all educated me but I knew there was more than that. Behind these scary numbers, there are people. They have faces. They have names. Each story is unique and deserves to be told and deserves to be known. That is what led me to write this book. I do not claim to be a professional writer, nor do I claim to have all the answers to the problems of this world. I write from my heart more than anything else. I take it as my duty as a human being who witnessed the suffering of others to write about it and call others to action. The book is a mix of my story in humanitarian work and the story of people who have been victims of war.

My journal entries form the basis of this book. I tell the stories of my trip and from time to time I put an actual entry from my journal so that the reader can feel like they were with me at the time the event was happening. I have purposely changed the names of the people who gave their stories, with a few exceptions. My humanitarian work is the structure for this book. I have omitted unrelated events. My purpose is to flesh out the condition of the people of Congo I want to flesh out the condition of the people of Congo. This is not strictly my personal biography. My friends might think that I have left out a lot of details, but this book is about revealing the humanitarian challenge of the Democratic Republic of Congo using my life and experiences. It is a chance for the voiceless to speak through me.

PART I: PLANNING MY COURSE

A Special Visitor

Growing up in Congo, I was awakened to the reality of injustice very early in life. Soldiers in 1990, who were claiming their unpaid salaries, looted the country. I heard my first gunshots when I was seven and the gunshots have never stopped since. I was an eyewitness of the pillaging in Kindu and Kinshasa. As a result of such violence, the country's economy fell to its knees. The collapse of the economy brought about poverty and political instability. Congo's society was slowly falling apart. The disintegration of social life birthed a number of social issues: street children, then the AIDS epidemic, which created a large number of orphans. Wars came along with cohort problems and social injustice mainly toward children and women.

As a teenager, I realized I needed to be a part of the effort to help these people. One of the first social issues that opened my eyes to the need for justice was witnessing the use of child soldiers. I was in Kinshasa when the rebels took power in 1996. The population celebrated the victory that brought an end to thirty-two years of dictatorship. Crowds of people celebrated their liberators as the rebels entered the streets of Kinshasa. The liberators were an army of children wearing plastic boots. My heart broke for these children my age who were holding guns that were sometimes as tall as they were. I assumed they had a difficult life even though I did not realize at the time how true my assumption was.

Many of these children came from the eastern part of the country where I was born. I wondered if any of my childhood friends were in the militia. Often the thought that I could have been one of them crossed my mind. We left the east just before the war started. The very thought I could have been one of them gave me a special burden for them. My burden was a stark contrast to how they were portrayed, as fearless children whose guns made them stronger than anybody else.

The struggles of child soldiers became more clear to me the day a young man came to visit my Uncle Gaston at our house. Houses in Kinshasa have fences made of cement block; a front gate provides entrance to the compound. That day, I heard a knock at the door. I went to greet the visitor. Our guest was about my age. He was wearing rubber boots like most child soldiers. He asked me if Uncle Gaston was there. I told him my uncle would be meeting him shortly, and I asked him who I should say was calling. He told me to tell Uncle Gaston he had a visitor from Kindu, a city in the center of the Congo. When the boy mentioned Kindu, it reminded me of the time I spent there during my childhood. I hadn't been there in four years. I threw out some names to see if he knew any of my friends. Unfortunately, he did not seem to know any of them. He told me a few stories in Swahili about Kindu.

I was observing the visitor as he talked. Although he was my age, he had obviously seen and done more than what children of my age would, or should, experience in their lives. He was still talking when my uncle finally joined us. They started talking about Kindu; they seemed to know each other well. My Uncle Gaston had been separated from his family for three years. He came to Kinshasa to get an education just before the war broke out, which separated him from his family in Kindu. He had no contact with his family because of the war. The boy brought news from his family in Kindu. He told him about his children, how they had grown up. He had stories about his son Isaac and the funny things he did. He also talked about my uncle's wife. Then they started discussing the war.

The boy told us he had become a soldier. He joined the rebel forces for money and for fame. He wanted to become a hero. He was told that they were revolutionaries and were going to be heroes forever. They were promised one hundred US dollars if they joined the rebel army. Our guest told us of his long walk to Kinshasa. He praised the rebel forces, and he had a well-rehearsed speech about the revolution. He told us he felt like a hero when he marched in Kinshasa.

Once he finished telling us the glorious stories of his military life, he opened up and started spilling the stories of his "real" life. He told us about the battle in Kenge (the gate of Kinshasa) where they had to face Mobutu's elite forces.

"I have never been as afraid in my life as that day," he said as his forehead furrowed.

He added: *"many of my friends died, guns were falling like rain drops on a roof. Bombs were exploding. They destroyed the bridge; we were trapped. We had no chance to escape. If I had a place I could run to I would have, but I was so far away from home. Even if I did have a place to go, they were going to kill me if I tried."*

Listening to that story made me realize the heroes of May 17th were the biggest losers of the revolution. My heart broke for him and all the other child soldiers. Even though life went on for me, our special visitor helped me realize I needed to work toward change in this world. I began to realize it is not fair that some suffer while others are enjoying a carefree life.

My adolescent years were filled with war, turmoil and instability; everywhere I went I found poverty and corruption. I knew that it was time to do something. I did not want to be a politician; politics had blindly led people to the disaster in which they now lived. I knew I could change peoples' lives by meeting their needs and empowering them. I might have been naïve in some of my dreams, but I know childlike faith and confidence has led me toward my goal.

The Plans of my Heart

Three years after I completed high school in the Congo, I received a grant to study at Ozark Christian College; a small college in Joplin, Missouri. I arrived on campus in the fall of 2004. My first semesters at OCC were the hardest period of my life. I felt lonely and isolated, and my meager English skills did not help.

I took fifteen hours my first semester at Ozark. I had a night class that semester called "Teaching Ministry of the Church." Dr. Doug Marks taught the class. One did not have to know much English to catch the passion Dr. Marks had for the subject. I loved his class even though it was long and tiring to sit through at the end of the day. I was trying to understand what he was saying, but I did not have a translator for when I was confused.

Dr. Marks wanted a fifteen-page paper for our first assignment. Writing these pages in English was a real struggle for me; in fact, I still laugh when I read the paper I produced. I was so frustrated about the work that I went to Dr. Marks to discuss it. As we sat in his office I tried in my terrible English to explain why I was unable to produce quality work in English. Being used to the Congolese way of education, I thought that Dr. Marks was going to kick me out of his office. Instead, he told me that he was going to accept the little I had done. He even added that I should write my major project in French.

He told me, *"Choose a topic that you are really passionate about and write your paper about that."*

The assignment was to be a project that described in detail how we would conduct a Christian educational program. The first thing that came to my mind was to create a center for child soldiers. I imagined a place where child soldiers would come and learn to be children again, where they would receive proper care and be equipped to face the challenges of reinsertion into the community.

Writing the paper helped me see the situation in the Democratic Republic of Congo from another angle. There were so many things I could not see while I was in DRC, because I was raised with a different kind of normal there. When you are on a tree, there are so many leaves you cannot see the fruit, but once you are on the ground you have a better view and can see the produce. Then you can climb the tree again to get the fruit. This is what happens when you are raised in a country where all you have seen is looting, corruption and war. When you leave the place and are exposed to another culture, you start seeing the differences.

When I was at Ozark Christian College, I lived in Williamson Hall. I discovered for the first time the statistics from my home country. I read an article during my research that there were over thirty-thousand child soldiers in Congo; the highest number of child soldiers in the world. Coming to the small town of Joplin made me realize how behind my country was in simple areas. Joplin had better roads than the third largest country in Africa. I always had electricity in Joplin, and never had to worry about not having running water the next day. These things were not considered a luxury in America, they were normal.

I began to wonder why a country full of minerals could not, or would not, offer these simple things to its citizens. The project turned out to be more than just an assignment; it became the blueprint of my vision to restore war victims, not only in my homeland but in any place that has experienced the same kind of situation. The paper ignited a flame in my heart. There should be no child in this world being forced to fight in wars that he doesn't know anything about. It is then that I thought it was time to change things. I realized that the change needed to come little bit by little bit; I started working for a better world. I got an "A" for the project. What happened in my heart while I was writing my paper was far more than the mere joy of getting a good grade. It was the beginning of a shift from words to action.

Ozark Christian College

My life at Ozark became easier with time. My English improved significantly. I was no longer isolated; I began to make friends on campus. My second semester in college was a blast. One day, I was sitting in the cafeteria listening to my friends John, Humphrey, and Katy talk. All of a sudden I realized I understood everything they said, and they did not talk too fast for me anymore. I became confident in communicating with people. From that day on, I started building friendships at Ozark. I was sharing my dream with all my friends. I kept telling them how I wanted to make a difference in Congo and all over Africa. One day while I was visiting a friend in Boatman Hall, I met Eddie.

Eddie wanted to know about my country. We talked about the situation in DRC, and I told him about the war and all the atrocities being committed in Congo. He asked me if there were child soldiers in Congo. When I told him that I just found out that there were a lot of child soldiers in Congo, he told me about a movie he had just seen about children in Uganda. The movie was called "Invisible Children." After Eddie told me about the movie, I wanted to see it, but I was so busy with school that I never watched it.

Meanwhile, I shared my dream for making the world better for war victims with each person I met. I wanted people to be aware of the situation in Congo. I was disappointed by the apparent apathy of the people to whom I talked.

I was surprised my friends did not even know where the DRC was located. I was even more astonished by the fact that they did not even know that there was a war on the other side of the planet that had caused three million deaths. I was upset and could not understand that people who had access to all kinds of information would be informed. I realized my first task would be to raise awareness about the condition of the people of the Democratic Republic of Congo.

More and more people were suggesting to me that I should watch "Invisible Children." I realized that unless something like "Invisible Children" was made about the situation in the DRC, people would remain unaware and unconcerned about what was happening there.

One day, my friend Williams and I were talking about the situation in the Democratic Republic of Congo, specifically in Bukavu. He told me about his roommate Derek, who made videos for youth groups and weddings. Colby told me to talk to his roommate about traveling to the DRC in order to make a documentary about child soldiers in Congo.

I began my preparations to go home and make that video. My first struggle was to find contacts to make the video possible in Eastern Congo. I looked online trying to find people who could help me to get there to make that video. I got in touch with a man at an NGO in Bukavu. We shared contacts for a while before he was assassinated in Bukavu. It was hard to find people in the East that could help with the project, and I had just lost my only contact.

The semester was coming to an end and it was time for pre-enrollment for the next semester. I wanted to take a New Testament ethics class, primarily so I would have class with Dr. Marks. I saw Dr Marks in the student center, and told him:

"Dr Marks, I have two of your classes next semester!"

"No, you don't." he replied.

His response left me astonished because I knew for sure that I pre-enrolled in his classes. He told me that he was going to announce in chapel he was leaving Ozark at the end of the semester. I was really disappointed because I was looking forward to taking that class with him.

Winter Class

I had to replace the New Testament class with another one in order to maintain my full-time student status. My friend Jace suggested that I take "Ministry to International Youth and Children." I was anything but enthusiastic when I went to enroll for the class. The class dealt with issues that children and youth face all over the world. My first day in class, I was sitting on the second row between my friends from Jamaica, Kenneth and Gilbert. When the teacher came in the class, he suggested everyone write their name on a piece of paper and place the paper on the table so that it would be easier for him to remember our names. I wrote my name on a paper and placed it on the table.

The teacher was walking, reading everyone's name as he walked by their tables.

He stopped in front of my table and said: *"Would you happen to be from Zaire?"*

"Congo," I replied.

With a smile on his face, he asked me where I was born.

"Bukavu," I replied.

It just happened he had been a missionary in Bukavu. His name was Mike Nichols; he had arrived in Bukavu in 1983, the year I was born. We talked about Congo all the time in class. He had a set of souvenirs from DRC that really made feel homesick. During the class, we watched a Dateline special about the war in Congo. The video had interviews of women who had been raped during the war. My heart was being emotionally torn as I watched that video. A feeling of rage was running through my veins, and a terrible sadness overtook me as I saw the disaster that was happening in the very land where I was born. I knew that most people in the room did not understand the gravity of what we were watching. In another class session, we watched "Invisible Children." The movie is about child soldiers in Uganda. It tells the story of children trying to escape from being abducted by LRA. It was a powerful movie. The song at the end of the video remained vivid in my head the rest of the week. I realized it was not only Congo that needed help.

Women and children are being taken advantage of everywhere in the world. Listening to stories of women raped in Shabunda, child soldiers in Uganda, child prostitutes in Cambodia, and other stories about injustice in this world was confirmation I was not going to make the world any better by sitting on a desk in the library of Ozark Christian College.

I did not want to take that class, but it turned out to be a great gain for me. I not only had my eyes opened to the injustice and abuse children and women go through around the world but I also gained a new father.

The very last day of class, I went and asked Mike: *"Do you have place in your heart for another son?"*

From that day, I became Mike's adopted son.

PART II: THE JOURNEY HOME

A Special Gift

Due to the elections, 2006 was probably not a good time to be in the DR Congo. Despite the tension elections were bringing in my country, I kept up with my preparation to visit. Derek, Lindsay and Jason were going to be my companions for my first journey home.

Once we had gathered the funds, we were ready to leave for the DR Congo; it was time to say goodbye to everybody. I went to see Judie, a lady working in the administration at Ozark. Ever since I moved to Joplin, Judie had been another mother to me. Judie had a special gift for me to take on my trip. We talked about how I was nervous about going back home; I did not know what to expect. I told Judie I had seen how people were treated different once they had been outside of the country. Sometimes people assume that they have everything in the world because they have been outside of Congo.

Judie is a great listener, she listened as I was talking about my hopes and fears for this trip. She told me I would be in her prayers all summer. Judie gave me my special gift: a bag full of envelopes. She made an envelope for each day of my trip. Enclosed were candies and scriptures. I was supposed to open them every day and read the scriptures for that day. Once I had read the day's scripture, then I could eat the candy.

After the envelopes, she pulled out another gift: a journal. This was the first journal I ever had. The journal was tan, with a palm tree in the center of the cover. It was beautiful; each page was green with palm trees on the background. I opened the journal for the first time and the inside page of the cover said:

To: Trésor
From: Judie
"To record how God works in your journey home! God is good! He is always with you! (And the others)"
"Write your story, "Judie said.

After praying for me, she reminded me it was important to write what happened during the trip.

Layover in Paris

The day after I talked to Judie, I left for the Congo. The journey started in a chaotic way; we spent the night at Newark airport before finally catching our flight to Paris.

Once we arrived in Paris at 6:00 a.m., the immigration officer refused to let me out of the airport, even though my flight was not until the next day at 11:00 a.m.; I was stuck in the tiny international zone of the airport in Paris.

I spent thirty-three hours at the Charles de Gaulle Airport. I met a lot of people from all over the world while I was trying to find something to do. One of the most interesting characters I met was a Russian lady who offered to buy me food if I would marry her. Later in the day, I met Pavlina, from the Czech Republic. She was a tall girl, wearing blue jeans and carrying a back pack. She seemed as lost as I was in the airport. Pavlina looked sick; she kept holding her ear as if it was hurting her. I saw how distressed she was, and I went to talk to her.

Pavlina and I became friends very quickly. We didn't really have another choice but to talk to each other; the only other people left in the international zone were a couple that spoke only Flemish.

Pavlina and I started a conversation that proved to be an important one for both of us. Pavlina was on her way to San Francisco where her sister lived; she spoke English and some French. It was her first time to fly, and her ears were still hurting from being in a plane. She was nervous about having to fly for even longer than what she just experienced. In order to help ease her anxiety, we talked about anything but travels. We spent hours talking about our lives. She told me a lot about Prague, her hometown. She told me of the beauty of her homeland. We talked about football, which Americans call soccer.

We walked all over the international zone. We got weary of walking and sat on a bench. While we were sitting, I pulled out the journal Judie gave me and we started a written conversation in my journal. She told me about how excited she was to see her sister after a long separation. I was teasing her about how good her

French was, despite the fact she kept denying she spoke very good French. She told me she wanted to know more about the Congo. She was very curious to know about the place I was going to visit. I told her a little bit of Congo's history.

I told her Congo is located in central Africa. It started as a private property of the King of Belgium, Leopold the Second. He called it the Free State of Congo. There was a lot of exaction on the population under him.

In 1909, the Belgian government took over the country and it became the Belgian Congo. It remained a colony until it gained its independence in 1960. The Democratic Republic of Congo experienced one of the worse dictatorships for thirty-two years under a man called Mobutu. He renamed the country Zaire for a while until he was overthrown by a man called Laurent Kabila. The country has been in war for the past decade and is one of the poorest countries in the world. Laurent Kabila was assassinated; his son Joseph replaced him.

My new friend was quite surprised to hear about the history of violence and instability in the Democratic Republic of Congo.

"*I do not know anything about the war,*" she told me.

She seemed ashamed to not know anything about it. I decided to tell her a little bit about the war. I said:

"*Well, Laurent Kabila came to power with the help of two neighboring countries. They did not get along well so they helped other rebel groups start fighting. The government had other countries come to its rescue. Then militias sprang up and it became complete chaos. It is an absurd war where no one knows who is fighting who and why. They fought each other and they are doing horrible things to the population. They murder, loot, torture, rape and turn children into soldiers. It's absolutely terrible, the crisis is beyond any understanding. To this day the death toll is over four million. People have called it "Africa's world war" because of the number of countries who fought that war. But all of them fought for the mineral wealth and all that happened was because of human greed. It is sad that our children have to pay for that and that so much blood has been spilled. The conflict in Congo is the deadliest conflict since World War II.*"

Pavlina looked at me and told me *"I am completely stupid."* She wrote in my journal, *"I feel that people in Europe in general just ignore all those things that don't happen to them."* She told me that she was glad I missed my flight because she was able to learn more about the conflict in my country.

Meeting Pavlina helped me see the power of a conversation in helping people understand what was happening. I understood that some people just do not know what is happening on the other side of the world. Sometime a little conversation is what they need to have the desire to take action. Pavlina and I exchanged emails but I never heard from her since that day. I often wonder what became of her. I hope she reads this someday.

Home Sweet Home

The next day, I finally boarded the plane to Kinshasa. There were not many people traveling back to Congo, the plane was half empty. I was anxious about the outcome of the journey on which I was about to embark. After eight hours of flight, we arrived in Kinshasa. Arriving in Kinshasa was quite an experience.

As we flew over the city, I saw images of the ground on the little screen behind the seat in front of me. Yes, I was back in my mother land. I was there to start something. I was hopeful and ready to take on the world. As the plane was landing, all my heart longed for was to touch the soil. I could not wait to see it.

I was excited about being home, but also nervous. I knew it was going to be hard. Things don't always work as planned in Congo. I was nervous about the way people would see me. How would they react? Would they try to take advantage of me? All these questions were in my head. As we were called to disembark from the plane, joy and anxiety mingled in my heart. Finally, it was my turn to go down the stairs.

The airport of Ndjili had not changed; it still looked like a building from another century, unlike the sophisticated airports I had been to in the past three days. The heat in the air almost burned my skin;

I had forgotten the grip of its warm embrace. Immigration officers in their blue uniforms were lined up to show the passengers where they needed to go. I had forgotten how everyone was loud back home. The military was ever present in the airport. Then I saw my father as I was lining up to enter the country.

The crowd was moving so slowly in this organized chaos, I instantly recognized my home. Dust and papers were everywhere on the ground. I remember the peculiar odor that one can only smell on the streets of Kinshasa. It is like a mixture of odors coming from dumps around the city.

Outside of the airport, I saw people walking. I had not seen that for a long time, certainly not in Joplin. Rivers of people, noise coming from everywhere, loud music coming from open air bars. Nothing had changed. It was Kinshasa.

But I had changed. Now I was home wanting to make a difference. My heart was full. I so wanted to see that place transformed. I walked in front of a street child at the airport, lying on the floor. I was reminded of why I was there.

Journal entry
Wednesday June 28th 2006

Yesterday we were arrested by the military intelligence while we were filming at the protestant compound. Even though we were out of that I have been personally threatened by the officers. They told me they would kill me if we filmed in public again. I don't think that either my Congolese friends or my American companions understand the gravity of what happened today. I feel lonely; my blood pressure rose after the officer told me these things. Nothing is working as I expected, but the Lord is breaking something to build some other things, I can feel it in the spirit. I call on you, Lord, to make this a learning experience for everyone.

Faces of HIV

During my stay in Kinshasa, I lived with my companions at a Protestant guest house downtown. It was far safer than any other place we found. There was a lot tension in the city because of the approaching elections. Violent riots from the opposition were common. One day as I was eating breakfast, I met Pastor Philip.

Pastor Philip was a Lokele like my mother; he quickly befriended me. We talked a lot about the conditions of the people. Pastor Philip told me about an organization based across the street that took care of AIDS victims. Although I had heard of AIDS victims all my life, I had never seen one. In fact it was not permitted to talk about AIDS in our home. I might have met AIDS victims and was not even aware they were infected.

My friend Eva was familiar with the organization; he had helped with a fundraiser for them. He gave me contact information for the resident doctor, Dr. Kamate. The organization was called Vorsi Congo, which meant *"widows and orphans of AIDS in Congo."* We made arrangements to meet and talk about their organization. I also wanted to go to Kinkole, a rural area in the eastern side of Kinshasa. They had a program for AIDS orphans there, and I wanted to see it. The next day we set out for Kinkole, a fair distance from downtown where we were staying.

After a long ride in the Baptist mission's Land Rover, we finally reached our destination. Kinkole is different from the rest of Kinshasa. It is more rural and greener than where I grew up. Kinkole had more of a village feeling than the slums of the capital of DRC.

As soon as we arrived close to the church, we saw a pastor waiting for us. A little crowd followed our car, curious to know who their visitors were. After talking to the pastor, the Vorsi staff took us on a tour of their working area. I was shocked to see the age of the children who were infected. I saw a set of twins babies who had AIDS. We interviewed a girl, nine years old at the time, whose parents both died from AIDS, and she was infected too. The doctors did not think she would live much longer.

Mrs. Neil, the Vorsi representative, also introduced me to a little girl named Annie. Annie was an AIDS orphan; she was only nine years old. After she lost her parents to the disease, Annie became mother to her two siblings. She had to stop going to school in order to be able to provide for her family.

Annie looked strong but she talked with bitterness about how she had to carry fruits on her head every day. She walked an hour to town and walked around all day to find just one or two US dollars to feed her siblings. Annie's dream was to be able to go to school, just like any child of her age. Annie looked at me with her helpless eyes and asked me to help her. I gave Annie ten US dollars but I knew that this was not what she needed to be happy. She needed her childhood back.

For many of the AIDS orphans of Kinkole, life is similar to what Annie experiences every day. They do not have any hope in the future. They need to be restored. They need to be children again.

Journal entry
Thursday, June 6th 2006

This morning, Christian and I were walking around the neighborhood just so I could get some fresh air. As we walked in front of the embassy of South Africa, I recognized a familiar face. It was Ingrid, my old friend from secondary school. She had not changed that much. We made fun of each other about things we did in secondary school. I realized that life did not spare us, we are getting old, and our stories are seven years old now.

After that, we went to the Vorsi office and the vehicle was ready. We had a long journey to Kinkole. I was afraid all the time on the road. I kept looking around to make sure no one was following us. I don't want to be arrested anymore. Being in Kinkole was a difficult experience for me. My heart is broken by the poverty in which my people live. I am overwhelmed for they are thirsty for God but their suffering runs too deep.

I still have the image of the girl they showed me, she just received a blood transfusion a few days ago and was in her final stage of AIDS. Should I come back to this place, I know I will never find her. Why, Lord? Why so much suffering?

Children or Sorcerers?

Our journey in Kinshasa turned out to be different than we expected. We were far from making the incredible video we set out to make. The political situation was volatile. I was arrested by the military intelligence because we filmed a military position. After the incident, strict rules were imposed on our filming project, which made things difficult for us. Despite those oppositions, the trip turned out to be an eye-opening and learning experience for me.

All my contacts in Kinshasa did not honor their promises to help with the video. I had to find other people to help make this project possible. A lawyer my father knew suggested to me a center he told me was run by a well-known NGO in Kinshasa. He told me I would find street children and former child soldiers at the orphanage. Because of what I was told, I was expecting to see a decent orphanage. The orphanage was in an area of Kinshasa I had never been to before.

The neighborhood was even worse than the one where I grew up. It was dirty, and the roads were terrible. Trash was piled like mountains on every corner of the streets. People who had never before seen Americans were following us; they were singing for my companions.

After a long ride, we finally reached our destination. It was nothing like I expected. Instead of a nice looking center, it was in a slum house. When I got out of the car and looked at the people around me, poverty was written on their faces. Their houses were in terrible shape. We had an audience there: children, many of whom had never seen a white man before were curious to see my companions. These children were malnourished. There was a lot of trash around the place and a bad odor was coming from the dumps around the neighborhood.

We were welcomed by the man in charge of the place, his name was Mayi Mobikisi. He looked like some kind of sect guru. He dressed like a catholic priest and had a large smile that highlighted his long black beard, stained with a few gray hairs. He had many disciples who revered him. He gave us a warm welcome to his place. As I walked through the big red gate, I saw countless children inside the little compound. There could easily have been over one hundred of them in that place. The children were running all over; they were excited to have visitors in their home.

I started asking some of the children why they were there. They told me about their lives. Each one of these children had a sad story to tell. I saw a little boy leaning on a white wall; he was wearing a red shirt and had the most beautiful smile in the world.

Cedric did not know where his parents were. He arrived at the orphanage a few weeks before my visit. Cedric was a handsome seven-year-old boy. He remembered living with his parents until his father lost his job. His mother attended a church where she was told that Cedric was a sorcerer. The pastor told Cedric's mother that the reason she did not have any money and her husband lost his job was because Cedric had cast a spell on them.

Cedric was handed to the pastor for exorcism. Instead of that, Cedric had to endure torture. Cedric's eyes were glowing with fear as he was telling me his story. Then he stopped for a little bit. He opened his mouth again, this time he described how his parents burned his hands with candles, he showed the scars in his right hand, and then he remained silent.

"Are you sorcerer?" I asked him.

"I had to say that I was in order to save my life," he replied.

He stopped talking for a little bit and started crying.

Cedric told me he went to live on the streets until the day he heard about the orphanage and came to seek refuge there. A little girl told me how the pastor forced her to sit on a burning stove in order to cast out the demons that were living inside of her. After telling me this, she walked away and went to play as if it was not a big deal to her.

I was overwhelmed with pain when I saw the living conditions of the children. There was a pile of mattresses on one side of the compound. I asked what they were for, and the caretaker told me the children used those mattresses to sleep on outside because there was no building for them. Children accused of sorcery were not the only ones who had sought refuge in that place. There were a few mentally disabled adults in the orphanage. They seemed to live in their own little world.

The place was so dirty and so hot I could not imagine how these hundreds of children lived in that place. I was also troubled that in the name of Jesus Christ, these children were being tortured. They were sent to live on the streets by people who claim to serve God.

These children's rights were violated. Every time I looked around the compound, I saw the most beautiful bunch of little ones. As I walked out of that place, I was shocked and upset about what I had just seen and heard.

We returned to the guest house in the evening. I was restless after what I had seen during the day. I went on a walk outside. It was a beautiful starry night in Kinshasa. The high rise buildings of the neighborhood had their lights on. There was little activity in that place that night.

An artist seeking to sell his art work to the expatriate came in the compound. He was showing his wonderful paintings to the people who live there. I walked to the little display, curious to see what he was selling. I was busy looking at the beautiful paintings he had when I heard a voice telling me,

"If he sells you that for seventy-five dollars don't take it, it's only worth fifteen dollars. I was born here I know how he operates."

She was saying that because most people charge foreigners a lot more money than what the product really costs. The lady thought I was African-American because she had heard me speak English earlier.

"I am from here too," I replied.

She introduced herself: her name was Lilliane, she was from Switzerland but was born in Congo, and her parents had been missionaries. She and her husband were going to travel the next day to Bandundu. We were talking about how dangerous planes are in Congo. Then we started an interesting conversation about my day.

I told her about my visit to the orphanage earlier in the day, I described the terrible conditions in which the children were living and the apparent lack of care there. Lilliane told me she had a friend from Congo who took care of children and would be a great contact for me. She promised to give me Helene's phone number before they left in the morning. After the long conversation, we parted; that was the last time I saw them. The next morning, I found under my door a note with Helene's contact information. I kept that number in hopes that I would contact her after my trip to Eastern Congo.

Journal entry
Saturday, July 8th 2006

Human suffering, an extreme poverty that put people to their knees, is what I saw today. This gives me the conviction that things can change and they need to change in the lives of Congolese people, especially children. Life has a lot to offer and we cannot let these people plunge into misery when we can help them have a window of hope. We cannot let this darkness destroy their souls. This darkness that turns the human being into nothing: he is a vacuum. They are convinced that they are nothing, not even God's creation. This is what I saw and heard there today. This visit was an eye opening experience for me; it showed me reasons I need to continue what I have started.

Journey to the Heart of Darkness

After a few weeks in Kinshasa, I set out to Bukavu to honor my promise to the churches there. I promised to come visit and comfort them after the war. Going to Bukavu was a very difficult task to achieve, mostly because the region was not easily accessible; there were no planes that landed at the airport of Kavumu. Since we were traveling during the elections, there were some serious concerns as far as security. Elections in Africa are not a peaceful process like they are in western countries; they are a source of turmoil.

I traveled with Jason and my childhood friend Christian. Before I left Kinshasa, my father warned me the region was not stable and there was potential danger as some war lords were re-arming. My father did not want me to go. My mother was afraid I could die there. My friends, who had connections in the secret services, also told me to not go. They told me that it was the wrong time to take a trip to that part of Congo.

But I wanted to honor my promise. I was determined to go, no matter what. I was perfectly fine with dying there, if such was my lot. This does not mean that I was not afraid. I was scared to death to go there, but I was determined to overcome my fear.

My friend Christian decided to go with us despite the dangers involved in the trip. He braved his fears and stood in faith with me. He told me that he would travel with me to the East.

"I have to go with you, I know you will not be able to handle this by yourself," he said. Then he added *"I will die with you if that is our fate there."*

I will always be thankful that he was by my side as I landed in Eastern Congo.

The plane slowly lost altitude and the thick clouds started fading away to reveal a wonderful landscape with a thousand hills. It was green everywhere. The landscape is breathtaking from above. I was in awe of the Creator's masterpiece. Landing in Bukavu, the city of my birth, was a very intense emotional moment. It felt like being back at my roots, where everything started. I was in the land where the first lines of my life were written.

There are no accurate words to describe what I felt when I landed in Kavumu. It was a mixture of joy, anxiousness and fear as we were flying over the eastern hills. My mind struggled with the reality that Bukavu is no longer the "Little Switzerland" my parents told me about. It is now one of the most infamous cities for human butchery on the planet.

The beauty of the green hills from above was breathtaking. I could see people moving around their little hut houses over the hill. The red soil of Eastern Congo was birthing a red dust as the wind swept over it. The airport of Kavumu has nothing in common with modern airports in the west. It does not have a tower; not even a building to welcome the passengers. Everyone had access to the plane, and there was a crowd outside the plane. My cousin picked me up from the airport with my two companions: Christian and Jason.

The airport is forty-five minutes from the city itself. As we drove on the dirt roads leading to the city of Bukavu, my heart was breaking for the place. Dust was omnipresent on the road to Bukavu. Houses, cars, trees, everything is covered by dust here. We discovered the lake, which was beautiful, but the dust on the car's windows did not give full justice to the place. People stared at our vehicle as we passed them. Their faces were marked with pain and distress. The military was ever present; soldiers were patrolling with heavy weapons in their hands. This was a reminder that we were back in a conflict zone. Billboards calling to vote for certain candidates were everywhere. The elections were in every mind. We entered the city of Bukavu the same time two of the candidates were arriving.

There was a crowd gathered on the side of the road. They were everywhere welcoming Vital Kamerhe, a native of the place who was running for the parliament. There was a lot of traffic in the little city and we were moving slowly. Another group of cars came, bringing Jean Pierre Bemba, candidate for the presidency. We were caught between the hoorays for Kamerhe and insults for Bemba. All Bukavu was unleashed; people were passionate about what was happening in their city.

Peoples' hopes were high and their expectations were great for the future of the country. They had faith that these elections were going to bring an end to the suffering and atrocities that war had brought to their land. They believed that the time had come for them to elect the president they wanted. This was the first time in Congolese history that they had a chance to do so. Everyone on the street wanted to make sure that his or her voice was heard. There was so much hope at this critical time in Congo's history. I was glad to be there at the crossroads of the Congolese history when an entire nation was going, for the first time, to have a say in its future.

The next morning Christian and I went to the Market of Nguba to find some bread. We met a friendly young man. His name was Heri. He kept calling me "Mukubwa" which means older brother in Swahili. I bought from him every day.

The same day we traveled to Nyangezi, located in mountains forty kilometers from Bukavu. These mountains portrayed the beauty and wisdom of the Creator. The road was red, so were the people (because they are covered with dust). We were on a journey to discover the deeper Kivu. We were fascinated by the beauty of these lands. There was a striking contrast between the beauty of these lands and the stories Papa Dido, our driver, kept telling us about the war and its atrocities.

We traveled through Mai-Mai territory. Their flag was flying everywhere. I asked Jean Pierre if we could go see the silver back gorillas at Kahuzi Biega, the national park. His countenance changed and his eyes darkened at the sound of my request.

"If you want to go there it's at your own risk. My church and I will deny responsibility." He said.

Jean Pierre reminded me that the FDLR turned parts of the park into their own sanctuary. They killed and raped at will in that area.

The ascension to Nyangezi was a painful experience. The look in peoples' eyes broke my heart. I read suffering and pain on the faces of the women I saw on the road as they carried heavy burdens on their backs. I could hardly see their eyes because of the dust our car was pouring on them. I felt bad being in a vehicle. Life and hope seemed to have departed from these lands.

The road leading to the church was so tiny that I did not think that the car would go through it; but the Lord was with us and we made it to the top of the hill despite the difficulty. When we arrived at the church, there was a crowd waiting with a lot of expectations. All of them wanted to see us and talk to us. The church building was burning with the people's passion. They worshiped in confidence and truth. I was asked to lead the seminar on "the light of the world". I had a great response from the people. When I prayed for them, I was transported in the Spirit. I will never forget that moment.

I heard that some of the participants walked through the dangerous mountains to come to the meeting. It is a huge responsibility to work with such devoted people. We had a meal after the meeting. We were served meat and fried sweet potatoes. The meat was the best I had eaten in my life.

The following day, our destination was Kadutu(a neighborhood of Bukavu). On our way to Kadutu, our guides opened up to us about their experiences during the war. They pointed at the hill where Kadutu was located and they told us that it was its own "republic" during the war. The Mai-Mai militia controlled the area and fought the Rwandan army regularly. They told us of the horrors they had seen during the war.

Our driver told us that he used to see corpses lying on the road all over the city. He told us how the Rwandan army did not show any mercy toward anyone who resisted them. I was deeply hurt by what I heard. As we drove, I kept looking at the people walking the streets wondering what their stories were. I will always admire the courage the people of Bukavu had to even talk about their plight. My heart was pierced by what they were saying. From that day, my life was never the same. The little naïve child died and the man who needs to act was born.

Tell the Story

I visited several places outside of Bukavu. I traveled from village to village meeting with churches and community leaders. I wanted to understand what was happening. Everywhere I went; people were living in unbearable conditions. The war had taken everything away from them. The people of Sud Kivu were walking corpses. There seemed to be no life in the green hills. I visited different villages, all of them broke my heart but one of them was the most significant to me: the village of Kidodobo. This rural community is located about forty kilometers from Bukavu.

I decided to go despite the dangers in the area. The next day my companions and I embarked in a journey to the rural village of Kidodobo. The trip to Kidodobo was long. We had to move fast, leaving a trail of dust behind us. The red cloud we were leaving was blocking the view, and we couldn't see what was in front of us.

There were fewer and fewer people on the road the further we got from Bukavu. The look on people's faces was different, and they seemed to be afraid of something. I understood we were entering an area that was not safe. As we drove into the mission, the cloud of red dust dissipated, and I could see a school that looked like it hadn't been used for years. Time and wars had left their footprint on the buildings in the mission. There were no windows and no doors in some of the places I saw.

There was still a long road ahead of us, and there was a beautiful building at the end of the road. My friend Jean-Pierre told me it was the mission. I was amazed by that building; it looked like villas I saw in other parts of the country. We had a little audience forming with peasants and children. They were curious to see the crazy people who came to visit their village. They were staring through the window as if they were intrigued about our presence in their land. After a long journey through the hills of Sud Kivu, we were in Kidodobo at last.

Kidodobo is a place of amazing beauty. The station dated from the colonial period, and it seemed to have kept some of its colonial splendor. The white building was a villa that was turned into a church by the early missionaries in the area. It was a white building with windows around the top. There was a hole in one of the windows in the upper part of the edifice. A rebel group came to loot the place and shot a rocket there. It was a reminder that we were in militia territory.

There was a very deceiving serenity in Kidodobo. The white walls of the church were obviously hiding a lot of secrets. The large green yard on the front of the church seemed so peaceful, yet there was unrest in the eyes of the peasants.

Before I came to Kidodobo, I was warned that the area was unstable. The Interahamwes, a Rwandese militia allegedly responsible for the 1994 genocide in Rwanda, were still operating in the region. My assumptions about the dangers of the place were confirmed when the pastor of the church told me he was kidnapped and tortured by the Interahamwes two weeks before my visit.

The pastor gave me a tour of the place. The building behind the church was a youth center. The missionaries turned an Olympic pool into a building that they used for children's church. I could see a few eyes staring from the houses on a little hill behind the building. The pastor told me it was the old orphanage. Children were there no more. They had abandoned the orphanage because they could not feed them.

Not many people lived in Kidodobo. A little audience followed us. We walked down the hill through the green grass and found a few houses that used to be missionary dwellings. Now there was a group of eight soldiers stationed there with their heavy machine guns. The soldiers had a few prisoners. They were Interahamwes that they had been caught in the area. After visiting the house, I was brought to the clinic. From outside, it looked like a lovely place; its past beauty still had some remaining elegance.

The clinic in Kidodobo was a magnifying glass that exposed the extent of suffering and misery in the region. There were people in the hospital suffering from all sorts of illnesses. Most were sick with malaria. I toured the clinic with the director. As we were visiting the different rooms, we passed by a little girl.

"*She walked on a landmine*," the director told me.

He went on to explain the girl was lucky the evil thing did not explode on her foot. We went into a room full of spider webs that used to be an orphanage for babies. The few cribs still there were covered with dust. I walked passed a group of ladies. I initially assumed they were sick but there was something about them that caught my attention.

I could not take my eyes from them; there was a pain in them that was obvious. The women were sitting on a bench with their heads bowed. Their Kikwembes (Congolese dress) covered their heads to protect them from the sun.

"*What happened to them*"? I asked.

"*They are vsv*" the doctor replied.

"VSV" stands for victims of sexual violence, the "proper" term to designate women who have been brutally gang raped during the war. Some of these women have been gang raped by fifteen militiamen. They have gone through the most horrible things one can imagine.

After I saw these women, I remembered a story my dad told me about a girl from the east who was being sent to Spain. She had been so forcibly raped that all of her insides were no longer holding.

I wanted to talk to the women, but I was not sure how. After a moment of hesitation, courage grew inside my heart. I asked the doctor if could speak to them.

"*Sure,*" he replied.

I went to them and told them that I was visiting. I told them that I wanted to know more about them. They were hesitant at first but they began to warm up to me and began to tell me their stories.

A lady in yellow was the one who spoke the most. She told me about being raped in front of her children. Ten militiamen gang raped her. They used knives and sticks and inflicted indescribable pain on that woman. Her lips were trembling while she spoke. Her eyes had a kind of glow, and tears were not far off. Then suddenly she stopped talking. I was petrified by what I had just heard. I was so moved that my heart was beating faster. The doctor, however, did not seem bothered - he still had a smile on his face.

I was so troubled by what I just heard that I asked the doctor if we could leave. I could not stand listening to any more. We had taken just a few steps when I felt a hand holding me with a firm grip. I looked back and it was the lady in yellow and, with a strong hold on my arm, she lifted her eyes to meet mine. She then told me in Swahili:

"Tell my story so that no woman will live what I have lived!"

She spoke with such determination that I was terrified and troubled by her request. I left the clinic to continue my visit but my heart was heavy and the words of the lady in yellow were still resonating in my mind. Before I left Kidodobo and its beautiful green hills, I stood at the top of the white church's stairs. The elegance of the growing flowers contrasted with the dark story I had just heard. The tea plantation nearby wafted a fresh scent to the mission. The pleasantness of being there was tarnished by the reality that the land I was walking on bore witness to the disturbing human brutality.

Now that I had heard the stories with my own ears and stared into that woman's eyes, I could no longer say that I did not know. I had to do something to change the plight of rape victims in that area. In telling these stories, I am keeping a promise to a woman who first opened my eyes to the horrors rape victims have to live each day. I will never see that woman again, but I will keep my promise to her. Through this book I hope that these people and their stories will no longer be seen as mere statistics.

On my way back, I wanted to see the Panzi Hospital in Bukavu. Unfortunately, there was a riot at the entrance of the road that led to Panzi, and we had to take another route to go back to the city. We missed our last chance to see the hospital. As soon as we returned, we had to pack because we had to leave early the next day. We took the boat to Goma, the capital of North Kivu. As we were in the boat, my mind was overcome with sorrow about what I saw and heard during the time I was in Bukavu and in its surrounding villages. We crossed beautiful Lake Kivu before we arrived in Goma to catch a plane back to Kinshasa. Goma was another place destroyed by the war and by a volcano. There were piles of lava everywhere in the city. The destruction of war was ever present during our quick drive through the city. As I sat on the plane, I knew that my work in Eastern Congo was going to be essential in bringing back hope to these broken people who had endured so much pain and suffering.

Journal entry
Friday, July 28th, 2006

When we arrived in Kidodobo, the atmosphere was heavy. Tension and fear could be read on peoples' faces. The Interahamwes looted the place on July 4th. The pastor told us what happened to him. He was very close to death. The Interahamwes took him and tied him with ropes and they were about to cut his throat. Someone else told us that there were two women who were kidnapped the day before. That news created an atmosphere of fear among us. The atmosphere was really tense in that place. The very few youths that came (we did not have a crowd there) seemed to be traumatized by the war. There was one girl in the audience at church who had been raped and her eyes only bore pain. The spirit moved me into a prayer of healing for these people. I asked the Lord to come and heal every internal wound in the people of Kidodobo. The girl broke into tears as I was praying. I could feel her pain deep in my heart.

Meeting Helene

After the experience in Bukavu, I returned to Kinshasa where there was still work to do before returning to the States. I needed to continue where I left off. I had to contact Helene, Liliane's friend. Helene invited me to her place to talk to her about her work. Christian and I went to Helene's house. She welcomed Christian and me at the gazebo in her beautiful garden.

Helene is an amazing woman of God and her smile mirrors her heart. She has a passion for children beyond what I have seen. She told me about how she gave up everything to follow a divine call upon her life: To help children and victims of sex trafficking. She worked with street children, housed abandoned children and helped restore child prostitutes. After talking with Helene, I knew that she was going to be a partner of my future work in Congo. There are not many people one can trust like Helene; she is the portrait of pure unconditional love. Helene took us to visit part of her work.

The visit was brief; we did not have time to visit everything. We saw only the former prostitutes she was trying to reintegrate in the society. I still remember the testimony of one of her leaders, a forty-five-year-old woman. The lady spent twenty years of her life in the streets until Helene rescued her and brought her to the center.

Helene's center houses twelve girls, working to bring healing to their lives. Helene's center is called Bongwama ya Mozindo (BOMO), meaning "deep change." The girls learn how to sew, pray, read and other important skills they need for a successful reintegration. Most of the girls in that place were trafficked in Kinshasa. They came from other provinces. They were sold into prostitution by some of their tribe members in Kinshasa. Most of them had resided in a dump in Kinshasa, and lived surrounded by trash. Helene selects twelve girls from the dump to come spend six months in Bomo. While there, they are empowered economically before being released.

Bomo was the first place I saw miracles truly happen in Congo. I wanted to see the rest of the work but we did not have time. Helene briefly told me of her work with street children in Kinshasa.

I left Helene that day with the feeling that it was just the beginning. Helene became "Maman Helene" for me, just as she was mother to numerous children in Kinshasa.

Unexpected Outcome

There were a few other people I met during this first journey home that became important in my life. One of them was a young pastor named Richard.

Richard worked with people who had leprosy. My friend Eva connected me to him. Richard came to visit us in our room at the Protestant guest house and shared his vision and passion for the lepers in Congo. He showed us pictures and talked to us about his work. He gave me important advice that I will never forget. During our conversation he asked me:

"How old are you?"

"Twenty-three," I replied.

"Do you have a fiancé?" he added.

"No I don't" I said. He then told me something important that I kept in my heart:

"You know my young brother, you do not drink, and you do not smoke. The devil will use women to destroy you. Be careful in your choice."

I remembered that all the time. It was precious advice.

My first trip ended with mixed feelings. Yes, I did not get what I set out to do; but I got more than that. I made connections that were going to last a lifetime. I learned so much and my heart became more aware of the issues I needed to work on in the Democratic Republic of Congo. The last person I met during that trip was a man called I Florimond; He was doing the exact same thing I was dreaming about.

He encouraged me so much about the work I was planning to do. He told me he worked in Nyangezi, a village I visited just before I left. He worked with street children in Kinshasa and war victims in the East. He was a Christian counselor, and I was studying to become one. Meeting him was a confirmation that my vision was doable in Congo. I returned from my first trip with the conviction that it was time to slowly starting taking action. I was decided to change this world one little thing after another.

Journal entry
Saturday August 10th, 2006

I am waiting patiently for my departure. I feel like I have learned a lot during this trip. I want to take advantage of each moment the Lord gives me with my mother, my father, my sisters and my friends. I am trying to rest a little bit while the tension in the city grows over the pending election results. I heard gunshots yesterday. They scared me. My heart is not used to that anymore. I want peace; I want to process what I have learned.

I hope all will go well with the elections and everything else. It is time to write a new page in the history of the world. It needs to be written with another color than red. We have seen too much blood. Hopefully politicians will understand that this time. I keep praying to the Lord for this country that I love.

Children on the road to Kidodobo

"We were captured on the streets. I was at home and we heard that there was a war coming. Everyone was trying to flee and I was doing the same. But I was not fortunate enough; they caught me and took me to their camp. I was trained and forced to fight. Those who resisted were killed." (Nathan, former child soldier)

Women in Kidodobo

"They found me at home. They raped me inside the house. I became pregnant. I gave birth to a child who is three years old now. We were at home when that happened to me. My friends ran away and I was not fast enough so they caught me. There were three men and one of them raped me. That night, they went in each house in the village and raped every woman they found. Only those who could run fast enough were safe. Someone helped me at first, but she ran out of money. Now I don't know what to do." (Beatrice, victim of sexual violence)

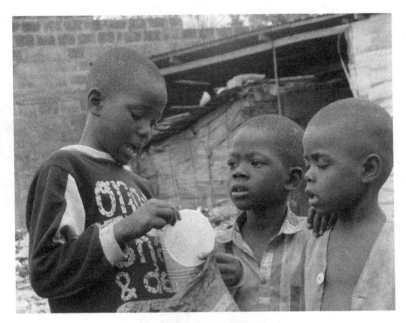

Children in Kinshasa

"My dad is dead. I remember they were shooting every day at that time. My sister was carrying me on her back as we were fleeing. There is a bullet that cut my fingers. I have lost my fingers. They raped my sister at home. I saw them. I was also hurt on my toe. I spent six months in intensive care at the general hospital. I am lucky to go to primary school."(Faith, 10 years old)

Aids orphans in Kinkole

"In 2004, Tutsis from Rwanda took me from our house and forced me to start carrying their equipment. They forced me to remain with them for an entire year. I went to battle and fought for them. I suffered so much in their hands. Luckily, I was able to escape. There were a lot of children who were fighting. We did not have a choice; we had to do everything they told us to do. In the military if someone has power, you have to obey what he tells you to do. Many of us were injured because we never received any proper military training. One day, they went to fight and the battle did not turn to their advantage. In the confusion and chaos, I left their camp to come back home. I found my parents, but they could not help me." (Charles, former child soldier)

PART III: THROUGH FIRE AND WATER

Fanning the Flame

I returned to the United States of America with a heart filled with conviction. I knew the change needed to begin with small things. I also knew that I wanted to return the next year. I had built a good base of relationships in DR Congo: I had Helene, Vorsi, and Richard in Kinshasa, and Jean Pierre as my main contact in the East. I wanted to research more about the issues I encountered during my journey home. Now that I had something to base my work on, I wanted to return for a better and deeper understanding of the situation in the East and in Kinshasa.

My contacts in Kinshasa were very close to the issues I was trying to address, but I needed a man in the East with knowledge of the issues there. While I was preparing to go back to Congo, Jean Pierre introduced me, through email, to a man whose name was Bahati.

We started exchanging emails, and I sensed that he was the man for the situation. He knew the places to meet the people in order to have a better understanding of the problems in Eastern Congo. I was now confident that I had a solid network in Congo. I was directing my energy toward preparation for my next trip to do deeper research. The 2007 trip was going to be a complicated one with a much larger group than the one I had in 2006. I was excited about the perspective of that trip; I had more passion for war victims in the Democratic Republic of Congo.

My personal life was being hit hard by my experience in Congo the past summer. I was diagnosed with Post Traumatic Stress Disorder two months after I returned to the U.S. PTSD became my struggle once I returned to Joplin. The nightmares that started in Congo followed me to Joplin. The faces and stories of the people I saw in Kinshasa and Bukavu were constantly coming into my nights.

I finally asked for help but relief was only partial. There was always a lack of peace in my heart. This struggle helped me identify more with those who had gone through a lot more than I did. I had experienced war and violence as I was growing up but nothing like what the people I met had gone through. I made a commitment that I was not going to give up on my quest.

I was researching and preparing to return home to Congo. I barely slept, which was not the wisest thing to do. I shouted my dreams of hope and restoration everywhere I went, but I became very impatient with people for their lack of action and understanding. I was young and crazy. I wanted to save the world but it seemed that everyone in Joplin was slow to move and help.

When the fight broke out after the elections in Congo, I was upset that no one even knew. I wrote notes and posted morbid pictures online to express my anger against the world. I realize now that this was not the solution people needed.

My promise to the lady of Kidodobo kept me going as I dedicated myself to tell her story. I brought back a VHS tape my father gave me in Kinshasa. It was a documentary that Médecins Sans Frontière put together about the situation in North Katanga. The video motivated me even more in the work I was doing. It angered me to hear the stories of people forced to eat their brother's flesh, or women who had been raped by the militias in that part of the country.

I read publications from Human Rights Watch and Amnesty International as well as authors like Collette Braeckman, a Belgian journalist, who is an expert on Congo. I had been reading her books even before I came to America. All this information raised my level of motivation. I knew I had to become an even better student of the history of DR Congo and the region in order to understand the conflict and its real source. I wanted to understand what makes a man turn a child into a soldier, what evil pushed militiamen to rape women, and why there are so many street children in DR Congo. Why would parents send their children to the street because someone says that they are witches? I wanted to know more about every issue that I had encountered on my first trip.

Women in War Zones

Just like most college students, I became addicted to the social media websites. I spent hours talking to people on Facebook or trying to find old friends. One day, I went on a page about the Congolese Diaspora. In the middle of all kinds of silly comments about musicians and dancing there was a post from someone called Scott. The post was saying that they needed help translating a video about sexual violence in Eastern Congo. After I read that, I kept trying to convince myself not to email him, but I kept remembering my promise to the woman of Kidodobo. I finally emailed Scott and told him I was willing to help. They decided to fly me to Philadelphia to help with the final translation of the video. When I arrived, I was welcomed by Brad, Scott's teammate. He had a big red beard. Brad and I began to work on the footage; we translated these videos everyday from early in the morning to late in the evening.

The video was filmed at the Panzi Hospital in Bukavu. Scott, Brad and Melanie, Scott's sister, lived there and made a documentary about the plight of rape victims. They followed two girls through their time in Panzi: Hélène and Bijoux.

They filmed these girls every day. My job was to translate every conversation into English. They were speaking Lingala, Swahili and French. Through listening to their conversations over and over, I became a part of the lives of these two women. I realized the depth of their suffering and the difficulties they lived through. I knew what made them laugh and what made them cry. I knew their jokes when they were with the other. I knew that Bijoux was a very bossy girl who did not like to eat the food sometimes. I became friends with these women I had never met, and I developed an even greater compassion for them.

While I was working on the video, the call for action became even more pressing. I wanted to do something right then. While I was there, I helped Brad and Scott make a few phone calls to Congo. I had the privilege to talk to Dr. Denis Mukwege, the director of Panzi Hospital. Talking to Dr. Mukwege was a dream for me. I was excited to talk to a man I consider an example and a hero.

Saturday night, Scott and I drove to his home. On Sunday he took me to the D.C area, where I stayed for three days with my friend Charlie. I was waiting to see my father who was coming to Washington. While I was there, I had met another online friend, Carrie, who became like a sister to me. Carrie was on her way to DR Congo for work. We talked for over two hours about Congo and what needed to be done to change things there. Our conversation fanned the flame of my passion even more. I went back to Missouri with even more motivation for my next trip to DR Congo.

A New Journal

My semester went very fast and before I knew it, it was time for my next trip to the Congo. I tried to be well-prepared for this trip. I even became a little more sophisticated this time. I had a nice looking prayer card with a picture of myself to remind people to pray for me.

Before my departure for Kinshasa, I went to see Judie. Judie had a picture of me in her office. We talked about what God had done during my last trip. She told me she had spent many hours making my envelopes this time because I was going to spend over sixty days in Congo. She had an envelope with candies and scriptures for each day of my trip. Judie also gave me a new journal to take on my trip. My new journal was black leather. It looked a lot more professional than my first one. The journal came with a blessing from Judie as she sent me out to save the world:

God is good!
He will protect you always!
Please record or journal about his goodness!
Love in Jesus,
Judie ☺
Summer 2007

I decided my new journal would be different from the other one, with not only my reflections, but also other people's stories from the field. I wanted to record stories of former child soldiers and victims of sexual violence. I wanted to make sure I kept their stories to be able to tell the world about their plight.

Scars of Kinshasa

My second trip to Congo began with a lot of enthusiasm. I returned to Kinshasa this time with the desire to learn more from the people I had met during my previous trip. Kinshasa had not changed that much. The airport was a little cleaner than the year before. Downtown Kinshasa still bore the marks of the brutal clashes that happened at the beginning of the year between the national army and Jean Pierre Bemba's militia. Bullet marks were visible on the walls of the high rise buildings of downtown Kinshasa. Some of the shops still had marks where they were looted during the violence from the beginning of the year. Even the cemetery had a few bullet marks on its walls.

We were in Kinshasa just a few weeks after the clashes that caused a lot of destruction in the city. People kept telling me how they lived through the violence, and how the fierce battle for the control of the capital had left marks in their minds. I saw images of the violence in Kinshasa when I was in Joplin; but driving through downtown, even after the violence had ceased, echoed of the brutality of the clashes. Many people were traumatized by the events. There was more healing to bring to the hearts of the war's victims.

The DRC was on the crossroads of history; its young democracy had many challenges to overcome in order to restore peace in the land. The newly elected administration had its hands full with obstacles. The population's expectations were great and its impatience evident. People wanted their needs addressed as soon as possible. They wanted water, electricity, food, and other things that they had been promised during the elections. People wanted to see a different Congo. They had elected leaders and were expecting these leaders to be working for the best interest of the country.

My companions and I lived in Helene's orphanage during our first two weeks in Kinshasa. During the preparations for my trip, Helene and I developed a friendship as well as a work partnership. Mwangaza Congo International, the organization I started, was helping her on special occasions like Christmas. We were learning from her as the organization was growing. Helene was in Europe visiting family and supporters when I arrived.

Helene's heart could be seen in the life she was giving to these children. Her orphanage was not some rundown building. She had built a two-story house for the children. The boys lived upstairs, and the girls lived with the dorm parents. There was not that much in the compound yet, but plans for expansion included a lot of games for the children.

They were fed three good meals a day and went to a respected school in the neighborhood. It was an interesting experience staying at the orphanage and spending the days with the children. I enjoyed being their counselor and listening to them as they told me their secrets. They always woke up early in the morning, and gathered in the play room, where they decided what they would do during the day. I joined them and we discussed the things that were going on in their little minds. The children and I also played a lot together. The boys thought I was a robot because I ran faster than them. Little did they know that I was out of shape in the world of grown-ups.

During my time in Kinshasa, I also visited the rest of the work Helene's organizations did. They work with street children in Kinshasa, and have different sites over the city where they take care of the daily physical and spiritual needs of the street children. We visited some of their sites during the time we were there.

I met some wonderful young men during our visit. All of them had stories to tell, but one of the most interesting was a young man named Elvis. Elvis is a very talented guitar player, but his family did not see him as talented. His stepmother accused him of being a sorcerer. She took him to a pastor who confirmed that he was a sorcerer. The pastor told the family to get rid of him or their future plans would fail. The family asked Elvis to leave the house, so he found himself at the mercy of street life for six months. He met Helene's people, and they helped with his transition out of the streets. Elvis had a dream when I met him; he wanted to record and release his own album.

Mouna, the French missionary who partnered with Helene, was willing to help Elvis realize his dream. He told me that he already recorded songs using a lot of different styles of music. Elvis kept telling me he was excited and that he and his band were good at what they did; he even gave me a little lesson about the different musical genres. There was another boy that I liked, his name was Trésor. He did not leave me for one second; Trésor wanted to hold my hand all the time. I never heard his story, but he became dear to my heart.

My last experience with Helene's ministry that week was going to the jail and to the girls' house. I had never been to the jail before. I had heard stories of people who lost their badges and were kept in jail. They were stuck in the jail because the badge was the only way to differentiate inmates from visitors. I was nervous that someone would try to steal my badge so I was ever watchful during the visit. We went into the teenage section of the jail. We had a testimony time, and then we shared a meal with the prisoners. The lady from the Catholic Bureau of Children, Helene's partner in the project, told me this was the only meal these kids would have until the next week. She was really nice, and we had a good discussion. She was from North Kivu, and was excited to hear that I was going to the East shortly.

Going to BOMO, the girls' safe house, was as heart breaking as always. There was a new group of girls in the center. I did not recognize the faces I had seen the previous year. There was a girl's story there that really touched my heart.

The girl was from Lubumbashi, in the southern part of the country. She was kidnapped and taken to the Republic of Congo to be sold to Europe through an international human trafficking network. She was rescued by a family friend who recognized her.

She was then placed under the care of an NGO, who then placed her with a host family. Unfortunately, her host father raped her and she became pregnant. The family was trying to cover up what happened, so they threw the poor girl into the street. She slept under a truck for a while before ending up in the center. Stories like that show how important the work of people like Helene is and how much it needs to be duplicated. She is truly the Congolese Mother Theresa.

The second week we went to help my friends at Vorsi Congo. This time we had the opportunity to visit their work at a small clinic they sponsored. I finally had the chance to meet Dr. Kamate for the first time. We talked about the problems of our country. He is a pediatrician and founder of Vorsi Congo. Dr. Kamate told me of his passion for people who suffer from AIDS. He told me his patients needed medicine as much as they needed food. He said clothes and food are good, but sometimes AIDS victims need medicine, and it would be helpful to bring medication next time. He had such a passion for the people he was around.

The Vorsi team took us on a tour with them. This was the first time I saw a man in the terminal stages of AIDS. I had seen the children in Kinkole, but this time it was at home in the center of Kinshasa. I did not realize that behind the gates of houses we passed there were people being taken away from their families by the AIDS epidemic. I saw the contrast between the dying man and the one who was taking ARV's and realized how these products could truly change the lives of those who have access to them. ARV's definitely make them healthier; there should be a chance for AIDS patients to access these products.

Vorsi Congo also trained us in AIDS awareness. We were not the only people attending the seminar; there were members of every church denomination there. All of them came to learn because, despite the doctrinal issues behind the AIDS epidemic, they had to deal with the reality that HIV does not spare any person or denomination when it hits.

I was encouraged by the fact that leaders were willing to do something to fight the AIDS epidemic. The church needs to be proactive in raising awareness against these diseases instead of pushing away those who have fallen victim to the disease. The seminar involved ways to raise awareness and teach people how to protect themselves against AIDS. I learned a lot during the training about the history of AIDS, and how it became such a widespread disease. Most importantly, I learned how to teach people to avoid the disease. I enjoyed joining them during that week, and it demonstrated even more that our working relationship would continue.

Broken Expectations

After the two weeks in Kinshasa, I left for Bukavu. We flew in a better plane this time, nothing like the flying coffin I took the year before. My feelings when I landed in Bukavu were different than the year before. I was broken by the conditions but it was not an unknown land like on my previous visit. There was some kind of organization compared with the previous year when we did not even know who was coming to the airport. We were warmly welcomed by the people of the church in Bukavu; the youth group came to welcome us. It was nice to be in the city after a year. I was looking forward to this visit. I wanted to know more about the issues and discuss with the people how to improve the situation for the people of that area. I landed in Bukavu with a lot of expectations and a heart full of good intentions for the future. Christian was with me, once again, along with a team from the United States.

There was a lot of traveling involved in the Eastern Congo portion of the trip. I enjoyed the first days of the journey until the trip became a nightmare. A few days after we arrived, I became ill from a local poison. The evil thing was in my veins causing me to vomit blood and wearing me out. I was exhausted and lacked energy. I was doing my best to do what I set out to do. It was hard for me to keep up with everything. The illness was such a painful experience to go through that to this day I have never found out who poisoned me. I really do not want to know who did.

I kept doing my best to do the humanitarian part of my work. I wanted to go to villages despite the lack of security. Because of occasional attacks on the road, it was always important to keep travel plans secret in that region.

I took my journal with me, and I recorded stories of people when I could. I wanted to give a voice to the voiceless. Even though the two weeks in Eastern Congo were not the best of my life, I did my best to give what I had left to make this moment count for something. I did not want to give up because of my sickness. I was not the only person who was sick in the world. Many people were poisoned in Bukavu so I did not want to be complaining all the time about being sick. Each moment after my sickness was a via dolorosa for me. It was heart breaking and disappointing, very disappointing.

A Visit to Panzi

One of the most touching moments of my trip was when I was finally able to go to the Panzi Hospital. I had heard so much about it that I greatly desired to visit the women who were there. I wanted to see the place because of the documentary I helped translate. I had an idea of what the place looked like because I had spent so much time watching and translating the video in Philadelphia. Unfortunately for me, I was sick that day, and I did not have the chance to learn as much as I wanted to. My heart was torn into pieces while I was walking through the common room where women with fistula were treated.

Watching these women my mother's age was the most painful experience. These women came from all over the province. They had been brutally raped by militias. A few people told me their stories. I was shocked by everything I heard. It is hard keep peace in your head when you hear those kinds of things. I want to go back to the Panzi Hospital and learn more from that place; the compassion that flows in that hospital is incomparable.

Where the Story Begun

I had an emotional moment when I went back to La Bote, the neighborhood where my parents lived in Bukavu. As I arrived, I had flashbacks of my childhood there. I even recognized some of the buildings, even though we left Bukavu when I was in kindergarten. Maman Marie, a Bukavu attorney whom I met in Washington, D.C., invited me to eat at her house. As we walked down the hill, Maman Marie showed me my parents' old house.

The house was nothing like the pictures I had seen from my childhood. The roof was collapsing, there were no flowers, and the windows were broken. I could tell that war and years had left their mark on the house. The people occupying the house were nice enough to let me in. They asked if I remembered my room; I told them I was only three when we left that house. It was a moment of laughter for everyone.

The house mirrored the city; Bukavu was not the beautiful place it used to be. People had built houses in every green spot, and the city bore the marks of looting and war. The town certainly did not look like the old post cards I use to find in my father's books.

Hope for Reconciliation

My trip was divided between church activities and humanitarian investigations. One of the visits with both activities was Mumosho. The village was not very far from Nyangezi, where I was the year before. The day before, I sat down with my guide and we made a plan. First we needed to have a seminar about caring for trauma victims, and then I needed to meet with Bahati, the pastor, who was going to help me with finding child soldiers and rape victims. I had sent word ahead of me to the pastor that I wanted to talk to rape victims and demobilized child soldiers. My plan was to do the seminar with the theme "If God loves me, why am I suffering." The seminar was designed to help war victims in these areas to reconcile with God and come to a point of forgiveness with their abusers.

Once the seminar was over, I was going to talk to the victims in person in order to assess their needs. The plan was to leave as soon as possible to go visit female child soldiers who were at a center not very far from there. I woke up with laryngitis that morning. We ended up spending more time at Mumosho and only saw the girls for a very short time.

The seminar took place at a small church in the area. We had a large audience as we talked about trauma. The audience shared their pain and the suffering they had endured during the war. We had a great response. My friend, Alain, taught for me since I did not have a voice that day.

At the end of the seminar everybody left except for those who were asked to stay: women and former child soldiers, but the room was half full of just women. There were women of all ages in the room. I wanted to talk to them about ways they could be helped. The women's eyes reminded me of those of the lady I met in Kidodobo the year before.

As we started talking, a group of men came into the meeting. They wanted to be heard, and they claimed to have been invited. After a short discussion it turned out that the pastor called for demobilized soldiers instead of demobilized *child* soldiers. Now we had a crowd with victims of sexual violence and former militiamen. I was very uncomfortable with the situation.

"What did I start, Lord!" I silently prayed.

Victims and abusers were gathered in the same room, and I did not know what to expect but I knew that the Lord was going to use this moment in a mighty way. The women sat on the left and the men on the right. As I was asking the women what they needed, the former militiamen were threatening them. They would not let the women speak, as they stared at them with intimidating eyes. The atmosphere was heavy, and I became nervous. In the midst of what was becoming organized chaos, my friend Alain proved to be a good diplomat. He brought the tension down in the room by talking to the men.

Alain reminded them we were there to help everybody and no one was there to intimidate others. At that point, the discussion became more peaceful. We asked the former militiamen why they committed such brutal and gross atrocities. One of them stood up and told me that the "spirits" required them to do these things in order to be invincible when they attacked their enemies. I understood that the issue was far deeper than just psychology; it was deeply spiritual. These men were animists; they served spirits that they believed gave them strength to fight their battles. The militias obeyed the orders of the witch doctors and performed any sacrifice the witch doctors asked them to do.

As the discussion finished, we offered both groups a meal. The tension was appeased when everybody had a plate of rice and beans, and there were a few smiles in the room. I did not want to stay there longer because I knew that the men we met were capable of attacking us because they thought we had money.

When I left Mumosho that day, I realized that reconciliation was possible if the offender asked for forgiveness, but that does not mean these men should escape punishment. I believe that they deserve a serious punishment for what they have done. However, true peace will only come in the victims' hearts when they will have forgiven their offenders.

The Fruit of my Father's Work

Jean Pierre told me about his friend Gratien, who worked with AIDS victims. He asked me if I was willing to talk with him about the possibility of visiting the work he was doing. A few days later, I met with Gratien. He shared with me his passion specifically about AIDS victims in the Sud Kivu province. He explained to me that Sud Kivu was a fertile soil for the AIDS epidemic because of the high number of rapes committed by the warring factions. He began to tell me about their process of rescuing the victims which involves taking them from their unsafe villages to a safe house in Bukavu. The patients were transferred to partnering hospitals in order to receive proper care. Gratien's organization is part of the network of NGO's that help war victims.

Their main program focused on helping rape victims with their reintegration in their community. After our long conversation, Gratien asked me my name. I did not have a business card so I wrote my name in his organizer. I gave the organizer back to Gratien. He had a large smile when he read my name, and then he told me:

"There used to be a man here in town with this name. I was in his choir; he was the most honest person I have met in my life. His name was Victor and you have the same last name."

"He is my father." I replied.

Gratien's face lit up with joy. He seemed so happy to hear that I was my father's son.

He told me of how being in my father's choir changed his life and made him who he was as a man. I was blessed to hear that my father was remembered for being a good man in the city of Bukavu, even twenty years after we had left the city.

I had vague a childhood memory of the choir my father started when we lived in Bukavu, but I realized in that moment my father planted seeds that had produced fruits. I was witnessing his work with my very own eyes. Meeting Gratien and knowing that he was in my father's choir showed me that investing time and energy in a child will impact the rest of his life.

Will You Take Her Back?

I visited three different areas at Gratien's organization. I spent the day at his office, visited the safe house and toured hospitals partnering with them. I asked Gratien if his organization was involved in helping victims of sexual violence around Bukavu. Gratien told me that they had a reconciliation program in Mudaka that mediated between victims and their families. Gratien invited me to take part in a gathering of victims of sexual violence who were evaluating the local program.

SOS SIDA was attempting to reconcile the victims with the community. The organization was able to convince some of the local leaders to participate in the reconciliation program, and their presence helped the process greatly. I told Gratien that I wanted to visit that part of their work. Gratien agreed to let me go there but, since he was leaving, Jean Pierre and two women from the organization were in charge of taking me to Mudaka to observe the meeting.

My companions and I set out for Mudaka two days after my meeting with Gratien. By this time, Mudaka had become a familiar site for me. I had visited the local church twice before. The roads to Mudaka are decent so the trip was short. We drove on the remnant of a paved road before we turned from the main road onto a dirt road. The dirt road led us to the center of the village. We drove through a banana plantation before we arrived at the meeting location. I saw a group of soldiers walking through the plantation. They had their weapons as if they were patrolling. I was staring them, trying to figure out if they were from the Congolese army or from one of the militias in the area.

The social worker noticed that I was intrigued by the soldiers coming out of the banana plantation.

"These are our soldiers," she said as I kept watching these men.

Then she added; *"The FDLR were here a few days ago, they kidnapped women."*

She told me that there was a path that led to the mountains behind the forest of bananas at which I was looking. She said that it was there that the FDLR, a Rwandan militia, took the women when they "visited" the village the previous time.

We had a special guest that day: the rain. It is very uncommon to have rain during the dry season, but the rain was pouring down on the frightened faces of the people of Mudaka. People were still under the shock of the FDLR's attack from the previous night.

"They don't come during the day," Jean Pierre said while smiling at me.

He must have sensed I was worried. I was concerned they might have still been around if they had visited the village the night before.

Our destination was a big wooden house in the center of the village. From outside, I could tell that there were a lot of people in the house. We were greeted at the door by a few SOS SIDA representatives. We walked under the rain and on the mud to reach the door. I was overwhelmed by the crowd when I entered the room.

Our gathering place had no window or ceiling, just a dirt floor. There was a sweet smell coming from the wet, red dust outside. Women of all ages were attending the meeting. An assistant told me there were one hundred and fifty-nine people at the session. Seven men were in the crowd helping facilitate the meeting. Every single one of these women in the room had been raped. Some of the women were freshly back from being held hostage by the FLDR. I was deeply saddened as I looked at the crowd, because I saw women who were my mother's age.

Since the secretary was not present at the meeting, I was "enlisted" to record the minutes of the meeting. I wrote carefully what I heard as they were discussing the struggles of the women trying to reconnect with their families. I understood the biggest challenge was that these women's husbands rejected them and took other wives. The women's families did not want to have anything to do with them because they had been raped; they were even accused of being spies for the militia. The seven men I saw when I arrived were trying to mediate between the women and their families. I was delighted to see people who really took this issue seriously. One of the men commented that other women were persecuting the victims, something I did not know. The man gave the example of mother-in-laws who were finding new wives for their sons and encouraging them to leave the victims. I could not understand why the mother-in-laws would not have any compassion toward these women.

At the end of the meeting we were introduced to the crowd. Since we were visiting, there was a question and answer session with the women and all those who were there. A lady asked me during the meeting why I was interested in helping rape victims. I told her of how I felt that it was my calling to help them. Another woman told me that she did not trust the UN forces because when she was held hostage by the FDLR, the militia forced them to carry gold on their heads in order to give the precious mineral to the UN soldiers in exchange for weapons. I think the woman thought I was some kind of high-up official and could make decisions that would stop these practices, but I was just a student. I knew no one would believe her even though I was certain the lady told the truth.

All over the province I heard stories from women about UN soldiers who were involved in trading with the militia, but their voices did not carry any weight and were always dismissed by political investigations. The woman had seen and witnessed what happened in the forest; but she was a woman, a rape victim, and Congolese, making her an unreliable source for most "intelligent" people of this world. Many other women who had been hostages of the militias confirmed they too had to carry the "gold" to a place in the forest. UN soldiers would leave weapons in exchange for the precious metals. I have no evidence to prove what these women told me, but I know these women did not lie.

The room erupted in discussion about the human rights abuses they had each endured. A man, who was standing at the door, came in and asked me, *"How old are you?"*

"Twenty-four," I replied.

He looked at me in the eyes and said, *"Let's say you were married, the FDLR came to your village, and raped your wife in front of you. Not only that, but they also took her to the mountain. She comes back from their mountain pregnant. Are you going to take her back? Are you going to love that child when he is born?"*

After the question, a heavy silence fell in the room, and we could even hear raindrops outside. All eyes were on me, as they were waiting for my answer.

These women were staring at me, waiting for an answer.

"*I am a Christian, and my faith and ethics tell me she was not responsible for what happened to her, she did not call them, she was a victim and I will take her back if she comes back.*"

I did not finish talking before the women started applauding me with the brightest smiles. Most men, however, remained quiet. I was a hero to these women, but a complete idiot to the man.

He shook his head and told me, "*You are too young, you don't know anything,*" before he disappeared in the rain. The controversial question brought our meeting to an end.

We walked outside after the meeting was over. The rain had ceased and a bright, meek sun was shining. I was greeting and talking to some of the women when a man followed me and asked to speak with me in private. We went behind the van so we could talk without the crowd seeing him. I did not want to go far from the group because I did not know what his intentions were.

"*These things don't only happen to women, they happen to men too,*" the man told me.

He told me he was a soldier in the government forces before the abuse happened. The Interahamwes captured him during a battle. They raped him multiple times and used him as a sex slave while he was in captivity. When he escaped from the Interahamwes camp and returned to his village, life was no longer the same for him. His wife left him, his family abandoned him. The worse thing for him was that no one was willing to help him. He told me that hospitals and charities do not take care of men.

Panzi would not give him free health care because it was only for women. My heart broke for this man. He was helpless and did not know where he could find help. Meeting that man showed me that the epidemic was actually reaching men too. It is impossible to even estimate how many men are affected by the situation. Male victims of sexual violence are afraid to seek help because of the cultural stigma surrounding them. The cultural consequences are so great they are silently dying from infections and trauma due to the abuse.

I shared the story with the social assistant who went with me to the meeting.

"*When Interahamwes realized that they had raped every young woman, they went for children, and then they raped mothers. Because they thought that most women were infected because they had raped so many of them, they began to rape men.*"

I was troubled by these words. There is an evil that is at work in Eastern Congo. Men will not speak about their abuse. We will probably never know what happened to the young men in the mountains of Eastern Congo.

The Kavumu Boys

My search for child soldiers was not over. On this trip, I made it a point to speak with and listen to former child soldiers. I believe the solutions to the victim's problems come from the victim himself, not from so-called experts who cannot understand what these people are going through. I wanted to know what they needed. I asked my contact to take me to places where I could meet former child soldiers.

My contact told me that we could meet in the small town of Kavumu close to the airport. A group of child soldiers who had been successfully demobilized were learning carpentry. These boys started their own successful business. I loved the idea of going to Kavumu and talking to these young men about their lives and learning if I could be a part of helping them someday.

Traveling in war zones requires a lot of wisdom and discernment. We had to keep a low profile on the trip to Kavumu because there were reports that the Interahamwes had attacked people on the roads a few days before. There was a taxi driver named Abdul who became my friend in Bukavu. He agreed to drive me, my contact and two of my companions to Kavumu.

The road to Kavumu is halfway decent; there are still a few parts where you can see the vestige of a paved road. We had to drive fast through the smaller villages because of the strong presence of the Interahamwes in the region. There was no reason to stop on the road. Outside of the main cities danger is everywhere as you do not know who controls which zone. The road was muddy and our small car was not holding up well.

There was a strong military presence on our way to Kavumu. The rain was pouring as we were going at full speed. We blew a tire one kilometer from Kavumu. Abdul decided it was far safer to keep driving to the city with a flat tire than to stop close to a bush and change the tire. He said that militias love those kinds of places because they can hide behind the trees and sneak in on people who are stopped. Kavumu is a city that is struggling between the wounds of the past and reconstruction. There were old buildings that still had bullet marks and new shops under construction. Kavumu is a strategic place in Sud Kivu, which is why fierce battles have been fought over that little city. The airport is not very far from the center of Kavumu. A lot of traffic goes through Kavumu. At the time the city was a lot safer than the surrounding villages.

We entered the city under a heavy rain while driving with a blown tire. We went straight to the workshop because we were late for our meeting with the boys. The workshop was a wooden house with a dirt floor. The old equipment they used for training was lying all over the big classroom. The boys gave us a little explanation about what they were learning. They seemed happy and proud of themselves for their accomplishments with the business. Most of these boys had been out of militias for a while and had a successful demobilization.

They told us most of the younger ones who attended their carpenter training center were not there yet because they were delayed by the rain. I talked with these men for about two hours. They decided to become useful to their community in order to regain the favor of their people. They told us about all they had accomplished in their work before they told us about the difficulties they had to face in their reintegration. Each one of them had a story to tell about what happened to him.

The guilt and shame for their past actions were still present in their hearts, and I sensed it when they started telling me their stories. I realized that even though their reintegration was outwardly successful, they had a difficult time returning to civilian life. As they talked about their past, I noticed that there was sadness in their eyes that told me that they still needed psychological help. I listened to the stories of all these boys, and my heart hurt for them and for the tens of thousands who were still in the militias.

Before we left, Keru, the teacher, stood up to speak. He told me of his passion for these young people. He said that he loved them, and he would do anything to help them. He was different from those who just reject children who have been involved in armed groups. Instead of rejecting them, he wanted to empower them. The Kavumu boys gained respect in their community by becoming the best carpenters in the area. The boys still struggled with their families at home. They also have a war that they still have to fight: the war in their heads. Even though they had been out of the militias a long time, they were still vulnerable to these problems.

Keru told me this, "*I love young people, and I want to improve my center. I want former child soldiers to come learn from me and have a chance to regain their honor.*"

After taking a picture, we left Kavumu. We did not want to take the chance of someone following us. I kept thinking about these boys and their hopes for the future. I know it is not impossible to give them a window of opportunity.

Finding Bideka

During my time in Bukavu I heard that there was a massacre in Kanyola, a village in Sud Kivu. I knew my next stop was going to be in Kidodobo which is not very far from the area of Kanyola. My friends, who have connections in the military, told me that there could be militiamen in the area after the clashes between the national army and the Hutu militias.

There was a rumor that the Hutus were now hiding in the bushes in Walungu. Their presence in the area made a trip to Walungu difficult to plan. I was still on my quest to learn more about what was happening, and I was looking for a place where I could meet victims of sexual violence. My friend Bahati told me about a village called Bideka where a group of victims of sexual violence were in desperate need of assistance. When I heard that, I insisted on speaking with them. Because of the potential dangers of our endeavor, we decided to keep the trip secret. The plan was to meet on the road to Kidodobo. I would switch from the van to his motorcycle, and we would ride to Bideka.

The next day, our driver came late and the plan could not be executed as we expected. My contact sent me a text message to tell me he was going to wait for me at the mission of Kidodobo. The road to Kidodobo was bringing back a lot of memories, but I was preoccupied about the rest of the day. I knew I had to leave to go to Bideka. I had never been to that village, and I barely knew the person who was taking me there. Most of all, I was afraid of riding on a motorcycle. Even though I was afraid about going to Bideka, I kept remembering the faces of the women who wanted to be heard and that gave me strength.

I was so deep in thought I did not realize we were already in Kidodobo. As soon as I got out of the van, I went to Bahati, my contact, and told him that I was ready. I jumped on his motorcycle, and there started my journey to Bideka. I took nothing but a piece of cloth to protect my face against the dust, my friend's digital camera, and my journal. I was sitting on the back of the motorcycle, holding on as tight as I could.

I did not have a good view of the landscape as we drove because of the dust. The red soil of Eastern Congo was all over me. Each time I was able to see someone's face, I noticed fear in their eyes. I had never been to that part of the province, and the hills were amazingly beautiful. I noticed a few children tending goats in the green pastures on the sides of the streets. I wanted to stop and talk to them, but it might not have been the safest place to do so. My heart was beating fast as we rode, and I wanted to arrive quickly. There was some activity at the bottom of the hill; we hit the place on market day. There were a lot of people and it looked lively there. We took a big left turn in order to ascend to the mission of Bideka.

Ten minutes later, we were at the gate of the mission. There was a big, dead tree blocking the passage at the entrance. A man came to remove it.

"The girls are waiting for you," he told me.

With a smile, he helped me out of the motorcycle. I had the hardest time getting off that motorcycle. There was a school further down the street, and the girls were supposed to be in one of the classrooms. I was nervous about meeting them, but at the same time I was amazed by the beauty of this village. Norwegian missionaries built the station as a base for their mission work in the area.

Bahati was telling me the story of Bideka as we were walking towards the school. There were several houses built for the missionaries and their families. There was also a primary school, which used to be one of the best in the region. Bideka even had a boarding school that used to be a place of quality education. The boarding school had such an excellent reputation that the wealthiest people in the area sent their children there. I was surprised the station even had its own car repair shop. Unfortunately, the war destroyed all of it.

The mission has been abandoned since the early '90s, when Congo started slowly falling into darkness. Bideka housed Rwandan refugees in '94 after the genocide. During the recent wars, different rebel groups used the property as a military camp. A militia looted the station as they were walking to Bukavu in 2004. There is a sense of splendor in Bideka, and excellence resonates from the remnants of the boarding school, which is screaming to be revived. In the middle of the station is a local church, the largest in the area. As I looked at the church, I prayed that this place would come back to life.

I Don't Have any Hope in Life

It took us fifteen minutes to get to the school because I was asking too many questions. The director of the school opened a room but it was empty.

"*Where are the girls?*" I asked.

"*They are there,*" he pointed to the yard in front of his office.

I saw a group of women sitting on the grass. Their heads were covered just like the lady in yellow I saw in Kidodobo the year before. These women were in great distress, all of them facing the ground. I could not help but think of my encounter with the lady in yellow the previous year. The director walked into the yard to invite them into the classroom. I walked into the classroom once all of them were there. I had tears in my eyes as I looked at these women; some of them reminded me of my little sisters. There was no expression in their eyes. Life had departed from their lives as peace had left their lands. Each one of these women had been brutally raped and taken hostage in the mountains by the militias operating in the region.

I was listening to their stories, and they were tearing my heart to pieces. Their stories were full of fear, pain, and despair. Most of them were from the area, they told me, and we were not far from the place where they were captured and raped. They showed me the hills from where which the Interahamwes came to attack their village. These ladies were helpless. One of them started laughing while she was telling me that she was sick. Her belly was swollen, and she did not know what kind of ailment she had.

"*What is there to laugh about?*" I asked.

"*I am laughing because that is all I can do. I don't have any hope in life,*" she replied.

I Did not See his Face

The ladies were helpless. Most of them could not tell their entire story because they were so traumatized. I also think that they were not willing to tell such shaming stories to a young man that they did not know that is until it was Aline's turn.

Aline was an orphan, both of her parents died during the war. She spent most of her time at a friend's house whose family had adopted her as one of their own. One night she went to her friend's for dinner. After the meal, she went to the outhouse where she heard strange noises coming from the house. It was as if people were breaking the door.

She called her friend's sister but received no answer. Aline was afraid because it was very dark outside. She finally decided to go outside and check what was going on in the house. She found a lot of people in the house. They were militiamen who came to loot her village. After beating the father and stealing the goats, they chose her to help carry what they stole. Because Aline resisted them, they became violent with her.

"The men started beating me up using their gun, I fell on the floor and they kept beating me. My nose was bleeding, I was hurting, but they would not stop," she said.

The militiamen took her with them along with thirteen other girls. Once they were far enough from the village, they started mistreating their prisoners. Aline began to shed tears, as if she was back in that moment of intense pain.

She remained silent for a bit, then added, *"They beat up the boys and left them for dead. They freed three girls after raping them. Then they started fighting to know who was going to rape me first. I was raped there. I didn't know who did it; I did not see his face."*

Aline was taken to an area called Ninja. She became the commander's sex slave for eight months. She became pregnant as a result of the multiple rapes. One day the Interahamwes were attacked by a rival militia, she decided to take her chance and leave. She succeeded in escaping the camp in the midst of a fierce battle. Aline wandered in the forest for eleven days until she arrived in the Bideka area.

I spoke with all of the girls in the room. The last girl to tell her story was only ten years old. She did not have much memory of what happened to her. Her innocent face could hardly hide the pain of what happened. She opened her mouth and with her soft voice she said,

"Dad died during the war. My sister carried me on her back; we were running as fast as I could. They raped my older sister in front of me. I don't have my fingers anymore, they were cut off."

I knew in that moment I was going to do something in Bideka for these girls. These beautiful girls have been robbed of their lives, they need to be restored and empowered.

Angel Made Soldier

I met him with his huge smile and eyes full of energy. Murhula is an adorable guy. Even though he was quiet and smiling, I could feel the struggle in his heart. Murhula seemed preoccupied. Bahati and I talked with him for a long time and he agreed to tell me his story.

Murhula had the voice of an angel. His name means *peace*. Murhula was calm at the beginning of our conversation and nothing seemed to be able to take away his peace. The calm did not last for long. We talked about the things that hurt him and he told me everything with a lot of pain in eyes.

Murhula was ten years old when he willingly joined the militia. Unlike others who are kidnapped, he chose to become a militiaman in order to have a better life. Militias promise wealth and dignity to those who join their ranks. Murhula fell into their trap. He went to the camp and was trained to become a child soldier.

During the years that he spent with them he was drugged up and forced to fight. He told me that there were many child soldiers in the militia; they were the first line when the militia went to fight. Not all of the children had weapons, but those who had them were first and the others followed them. Many of these children died in battle. When Murhula realized that he made a mistake he decided to run away.

One day he told some of his fellow child soldiers that he was going to the village to buy them a drink. The others agreed to keep his weapon for him. He went to the village, then fled to go back home. I asked him if he had killed someone during the war.

He answered, *"I had a weapon. I hate the militia because of war."*

I sensed that his heart was heavy and offered to take a walk with him around the mission. We arrived at one of the houses in the station; it was the one Bahati occupied during his travels.

"Can you write in French?" I asked Murhula.

"Yes I can," he said.

I asked Bahati to help Murhula write down his story for me because I wanted him to write it for himself.

I told Murhula, *"I would like for you to write everything you remember about your life in the militia. Give the story to papa Bahati. He will send me your story--you are going to be in my book!"*

A Child Again

Meeting Murhula was one of the best things that happened to me in the Congo. In him, I saw the transformation I have always dreamed of for other child soldiers. Also, Murhula's parents are examples of what parents' responses should be. They welcomed their child back into their home instead of abandoning him. They helped Murhula through his difficult transition out of the militia.

His parents' unconditional love was the key to Murhula's re-integration. I am blessed to have met that young man. I left Bideka with a heart full of hope for the future, even though I knew there was nothing I could do at the time. From that day on, Bideka became my first healing center in Eastern Congo. It is a place of hope that deserves to be revived.

Murhula is an example of the kind of transformation that can happen in a former child soldier.

The director of the school told me, *"If you had seen him when he first came out of the army you would not think you were sitting with the same person."*

Just like every other child soldier I had met, Murhula had a struggle with his re-integration in the community. Murhula had a lot of disciplinary problems at school. In addition, people did not like him because he was a former child soldier. Although he faced many challenges in his re-integration, Murhula succeeded in making the transition. The young man sitting in front of me led the choir at the CELPA church in Bideka. He was trying to go back to school even though there was no money. It is that struggle for a new life that I saw in Murhula that made me say a prayer of blessing over him. Once Bahati and I finished talking with Murhula, we walked to the houses in the property. I held his hand as a sign of endearment towards him. I talked to him as we walked, and I asked him what he wanted to do.

"I want to become a doctor," he said, with a big smile on his face.

Sorrowful End

The summer was over for me the day I became ill in Bukavu. And, there was not that much I could do after I returned to Kinshasa. I did my best to remain strong but my sickness was really affecting me and I never recovered from it. I returned to Kinshasa very sick. I really thought I would die in the plane. I always thought I was not afraid of death, but when I saw its face, I was terrified by it.

"I can't function anymore." I thought

No one could tell what was going on.

I was so touched by the love my American friends showed me. Kenny sent me some money to help with my hospital bill. Nathan Stang texted me to say he was praying for me. It was such a blessing to know that someone was praying for me. Each morning I received prayers via text message from Tonia.

I talked to my friend Keith and he told me, *"We love you and miss you"*.

I talked to Vernon and Lucille (my dear host family in the U.S.) to reassure them that I was still alive. Shannon told me that Jace wanted to fly to Congo and take care of me. It was great to know that people actually cared about me even though I felt misunderstood by some.

This episode plunged me into a time of doubt. I often wondered why things could not go back to the way they were. Back to when I did not have any doubt about God's goodness. Even though I doubted, I knew the Lord would prove himself. I prayed that God would raise me up because the enemy had struck me hard, and I was deeply hurt.

Journal entry
Tuesday August 7th, 2007

I don't know what to think about all this. Has God abandoned me? Why am I going through this? I want to find the strength to live again, but for sure things are never going to be the same again in my heart. I am hurt, deeply hurt, but God makes a way and I will come back and continue my work. It does not matter how or with whom, I will come back and finish what I have started. The devil will not win. Dear God, You will have to shake my world and show me something awesome next year because I don't like what is happening. You will have to open a new way of doing things, for I want Your Spirit to lead. I don't want to do this by myself anymore. Lead, Holy Spirit.

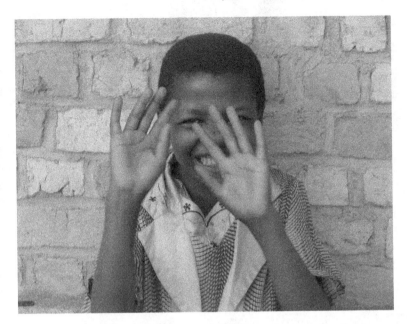

A girl in Mudaka

"The Interahamwes found us as we were spending time as a family. They kidnapped us for two months. Once we reached the camp, they forced us to cook for them. I am lucky I did not get pregnant when I was there. One day they went to fight and we fled from their camp. My parents helped me and welcomed me back. A lady felt sad for me and helped me. I am physically healed but I still have problems in my head. I am traumatized. I would love to be independent, maybe get a loan to get some land and start a small garden so I can have an income." (Mireille, Victim of sexual violence)

Children at an orphanage

"I became a child soldier at the age of seven. They used me to carry heavy burdens. I trained in Kalehe. We had to wear military uniforms and carry guns. I fought many battles and did many things that I am afraid to talk about now. We were a group of 21 children. I stayed there in the militia in Kalehe until the government's forces conquered the area. It was so cold that many of my friends became sick. It is not easy for little children to sleep in the forest every day. During the battle, I ran away and came to Kavumu. I just want another chance in life." (Kevin, former child soldier)

PART IV: FROM DOUBT TO A PLACE OF ABUNDANCE

Binding the Broken Heart

My return to Joplin was not easy. I was sick and bitter about the summer. No one could diagnose my illness. I was wondering if I was going to make it or not. Life is different after you have stared death in the eye; you realize you are not as strong as you think. The month after I returned to Joplin was the hardest time of my life. My sickness was devouring me physically and emotionally. I was deeply affected by my condition.

My host parents took me to a natural doctor in Grove, Oklahoma, Dr. Paula Rochelle. The day I met with Dr. Paula, she looked me in the eyes and told me:

"I have no idea of what you have."

I was filled with despair when I heard these words. I thought I was surely going to die. But then Dr. Paula looked at me with a smile on her face and said:

"I am a better doctor than that."

Dr. Paula was a great doctor indeed. She used her skill to heal my sickness. Dr. Paula gave me medicines to stop the bleeding. I thank God for her! I was on the mend for a long time. All the while, I was taking a multitude of medicines that had two things in common: nasty taste and terrible smell. Even though these medicines were nasty, they brought healing to my body. In addition to the medicines, I was on a strict diet for a while. I could not eat any of my favorite foods. Yet all the while my friends surrounded me with love and comfort during those painful moments. My friend Gabriel even flew to Joplin to visit me. I felt the comfort of having a brother with me when all this was happening. I am thankful for those who showed me so much affection during my sickness.

I was not only trying to win the battle with the sickness in my body, but I was also fighting another battle in my head every day. PTSD made a comeback in my life, and I had many sleepless nights because of anxiety.

The truth was that I had been so close to death that it was just now hitting me. I was always thinking about what would have happened if I did not find help. The situation not only affected my social life but also my school work. I took eighteen credit hours that semester, which did not help my recovery at all. I was lacking energy and concentration in school. Every day was a battle in my head, just like the child soldiers I had met in the Democratic Republic of Congo. Because of my sickness, that semester was my worst semester at Ozark Christian College. My grades were terrible, and I did not recognize myself when my grade report came. I was disappointed with myself.

The crisis did not spare my social life either. I ceased to be the social butterfly I had always been at Ozark. I was no longer the darling of the college hallways. I spent most of my time at my house. I just wanted to spend time with my host parents, Vernon and Lucille, and the children who came to their day care. The children had always brought a ton of joy in my life, and I played with them all the time. We had some deep conversations, I shared my ideas with them, and it was my only source of fun.

My faith was also deeply challenged by everything happening in my life. I was angry at the world and at God. I could not understand why someone would try to take my life when I was trying to help them. Several times during this period, I thought of quitting everything and giving up. My heart was wounded by what happened during the summer. I spent a lot of time thinking through the situation.

Worship was the only thing helping me hold on to what I was doing. I did not always feel like it, but I knew that God was God and He knew what He was doing. He had bailed me out of the worst situations, so why would He not do it this time? I worshipped even though I did not always feel like praising Him, because I knew something was wrong with me and I needed God's help to fix it.

The crisis turned into an opportunity to define who I am in Christ and who I wanted to become. In times of hardship, pain, and betrayal we have two choices: put our trust in God or forget Him and fall into complete darkness. It was only when I had found my true identity in Christ that I renewed my commitment to follow Christ wherever He would send me in the world. I decided to obey His call to work with the poor and oppressed wherever they are, starting in the DRC. I made a clear commitment to work for hope and change in the lives of the poor and the oppressed in the world no matter what. I would press toward that goal no matter what the cost.

Journal entry:
September 20th, 2007

"O Thou Tender Silence, speak as I go into silence. Speak the word that will release me and heal me and make me adequate. I consent without reservation to the draining of every swamp of self-centeredness and fear. Clean me out to my depths. For the world is sick and I want to be a part of the cure instead of the disease." (E. Stanley Jones)

Ready for a New Adventure

Once I had a clear commitment to work for the poor and the oppressed in the world, I spent hours writing the vision I had for the future. I detailed for myself what I wanted to accomplish. I wanted to make the time God had given me count for something. I clearly defined on paper what the vision of the work in Congo and in the rest of the world would be.

Once I had finished writing my vision, I decided to do a deep introspection and decide what kind of man I needed to be. I wrote these things on a paper and posted it in my room. Writing these two papers was like a road map for my life. I needed one more trip to Congo before I started working there. I needed confirmation about what I was doing. I wanted to be able to see it before I decided on an action plan. Meanwhile, the Spirit was slowly opening things in my mind about the work I had to accomplish in Congo.

I began to prepare for my 2008 trip in December 2007. I considered it my last research trip to the Democratic Republic of Congo before I officially started working there. While I was preparing my trip, I was convicted to take this trip by myself. I wanted to go and see things for myself this time. I prayed specifically that God would make this trip an experience that would shake my world. I desperately wanted to see a miracle. One day, my friend and sister Carrie sent me an email from Kinshasa telling me her parents were going to visit her in Congo during the summer. Carrie told me she would love for me to help them find something to do that could help the people while they were in Kinshasa.

I emailed Dr. Joe, Carrie's dad, to get in touch with him and see how I could help them during their trip. Dr. Joe told me he wanted to visit children in Congo. He is a plastic surgeon and had heard of Mutombo Dikembe's hospital in Kinshasa and wanted to visit it. I was so excited he wanted to visit Congo that I decided I would make sure I was there to meet them. I made it an important part of my trip. Getting ever more organized in my preparation, I sent out support letters to raise funds for the trip early in 2008. Around the same time, I also finished mapping my trip to Congo. I was revived in my spirit, and I was feeling better physically and spiritually. I was very much alive, feeling my passion return, as I became ready to take on the world.

Mike Nichols came to teach a winter class in Joplin in January 2008. Mike and I met when he came to teach the same class in 2006. We had a good visit while he was in Joplin, and Mike encouraged me a lot. He even let me discuss social issues in his class. Mike was going back to Congo for the first time since he left in the early nineties. I was convinced it was God's Divine plan for me to travel with him, and this made me impatient and more excited for the trip. We made plans while he was in Joplin. Mike's visit was a blessing to me, since I was feeling now that everything was back in place with my life.

Spring 2008 turned out to be a great semester for me: I was back to the man I was before Summer 2007. The smile I lost in Bukavu was back on my face. The energy and enthusiasm the poison stole from me was back in my heart. I was excited about life, and worship was back in my heart. I enjoyed each day of my life that semester.

Journal entry:
Friday, October 26th, 2007

"Proverb 11" man (from Mike):
1. Man of Honesty
2. Man of Humility
3. Man of Integrity
4. Man of Justice
5. Man of Trust
6. Man of Kindness
7. Man of Generosity

Reconnecting

As I made it a point to become a student of the world, not only did I study the conflict in Congo but I also studied the rest of the world. I was learning more about the world we live in and was creating a network of friends all over the world for future work. Even though I was looking on the global aspect of my future work, the Democratic Republic of Congo was my present concern. I was diligently keeping in touch with my people in Congo, as we began preparing for my next visit.

It was time to reactivate old relationships in the region. I was reassuring my friends that I was not upset with anyone for what happened in 2007. Most of my partners felt responsible for what happened to me. However, I encouraged them to put these events in the past. The time had come for us to work toward our goals. I realized that I needed to spend time with them as friends instead of just seeing them as business partners. During this time, I was doing a lot of research, and writing reflections about what I found in my leather journal. I became a self-taught student of the humanitarian situation in Congo.

War in the East

The situation in Congo was slowly becoming a source of concern. Tension was rising in the East as residual militias were trying to conquer the North Kivu province, and Laurent Nkunda, a rebel, was attacking again. Hope was fading after the elections because war was back in Eastern Congo. To stay updated, I read the news online and I listened to the radio every day. News reports were saying that Nkunda's troops were defeating the national army, and pictures of Congolese refugees were back on the news sites. Everyone thought the elections would end the wars, but selfish political ambitions were destroying the hopes of the population. The river of war-stained blood was flowing again in Eastern Congo.

Soon Nkunda's rebels were thirty kilometers from Goma, making my visit to Goma harder to plan. Nobody knew when the rebels would attack the city, and many reports stated that Laurent Nkunda's troops were using child soldiers. Such news was disheartening, as I watched the situation go from bad to worse. To me, it seemed that all the progress made to stop the use of child soldiers was annihilated. According to my friends in Goma, demobilized child soldiers were the primary target of Nkunda's troops. My heart began to hurt for these children, for it appeared that they were on a cycle that they could not break. This was a reminder that the situation of child soldiers deserved more attention. With the rising tension in the East, I knew my trip was going to be eventful.

Closed Doors

Once school was out, I began to make the final preparations for my trip to the Democratic Republic of Congo. I wanted to meet with Mike in Bukavu after being in Kinshasa, then I would come back to meet with my partners to help them as much as possible in their work in Kinshasa.

Everything was ready on paper; all I needed to do was wait for the funds for the trip. I was waiting impatiently for June to come so I would be in Congo, but I was having a problem: Out of the several thousand dollars I needed for the trip, I had only raised $100 over the past six months. I was growing nervous as the days went by without funds for my trip to Congo. My friend Mike left for DRC, and I was still in Joplin waiting to get the money to join him.

I was still hoping that somehow divine financial provision would fall on me. I emailed Mike several times while he was in DR Congo to tell him how I wanted to be in Bukavu. I was telling him in my emails that I longed to walk the streets of Bukavu with him. Each day I prayed that some kind of miracle would happen for me to be able to go to Congo; but nothing was happening.

Instead of the blessing I was expecting, the doors were closing one after another. I tried to be patient but I was frustrated. I did not understand why all this was happening to me. I kept praying that something would work out but it seemed like my prayers were vain. Mike came back from the Democratic Republic of Congo, and I was still in Joplin waiting for my trip. I had to erase activity after activity from my to-do list in Congo as their dates were passing by while I waited in Joplin. I began wondering if I would be able to make it that summer with only a hundred dollars raised for the trip.

Time passed, and I became even more disappointed that my prayers were not answered. I sent an email asking all my friends to pray for me because I was losing hope. I received a lot of prayers and love from those who received the email. My friends encouraged me to keep praying. I was now wondering whether or not God wanted me to go to Congo. It was almost the end of June and I still did not have any money to go on my trip.

In the midst of my frustration, my friend Adam encouraged me every day on Facebook, for he was sure I would go to Congo that summer. Adam reminded me I needed to wait for God's time. Dr. Gary Zustiak, my professor of psychology, sent me an email encouraging me to be patient and wait on God to move. He even sent me a presentation he made for a class he was teaching on the book of Nehemiah. He told me that when the timing was right, God provided everything Nehemiah needed for the work He wanted him to do. Not only did Nehemiah receive the provision, but God also gave him protection to go where He was sending him.

I was encouraged by the message and the email, but I still thought there was not enough time left for something significant to happen during my trip to Congo. I had spent most of my summer chasing funds without success. I gave a challenge to God in my prayers about the funds; I told him I wanted to have a specific amount of money by a specific day. I told God I would not believe He wanted me to go unless He provided the money.

(Email from Dr. Zustiak:)
Saturday, June 14th 2008

Dear Tresor,

I am so sorry to hear that your plans are not working out as you had originally hoped. I know that you put a lot of thought and prayer into your lessons and what would be most helpful for you to share. Surely this is a discouraging time for you, but I would encourage you to trust in the Lord and wait on him to open the doors. When Nehemiah desired to travel back to Jerusalem and rebuild the walls, he prayed and fasted for 4 months before God opened the doors. But, when God's timing was ready, not only was Nehemiah allowed to have the time off, but the King and Queen supplied him with all of the needed resources, authority and protection in travel. My good friend J.K. Jones used to say, "God is never late, but He is seldom early." Rom 8:28 my friend. I will continue to pray for you and that your heart will be encouraged and strengthened.

Zus

Divine Provision

I issued a challenge to God in my prayers. I was expecting Him to prove Himself up to the challenge. Monday morning I was praying God would multiply the hundred dollar check I received from Unity Baptist Church. I held the check and prayed for a miracle that day. After my prayer, I went downstairs to read my emails. I was certain to find emails from everybody in Congo wondering why I kept pushing my trip back. My contacts and my family wondered if they should continue preparing for my arrival since I had been postponing the trip. Everything was uncertain. I could not commit to any plans since I did not know when I was going to leave the United States. I did not even know if I *was* going to leave. In the midst of the emails from Congo, I found an email from a dear friend of mine saying:

"I have some financial questions for you about your trip, so if you could give me a call as soon as possible I would appreciate it. I left a message on your phone, but I thought you might check your email first."

After I read the email, I ran quickly upstairs to find my phone and listen to the message. My hands were shaking as I listened to the message. I had a feeling God was about to respond to my challenge. I listened to the message, and the brother was telling me he and his family were willing to give me 75 percent of my challenge to God. I was so excited after our phone call, it sounded like things were finally being set into motion. I jumped up and down with joy because I knew nothing was going to stop what God had started. My heart was filled with joy and hope. I knew that I was going to Congo. I received the phone call from my friend at ten o'clock in the morning. Miracles started happening. Someone gave me two hundred dollars at eleven thirty, the Lord had provided the thousand dollars I asked for before noon.

Now I knew I had divine permission and provision for this trip, and I had to restructure the trip because I had missed all my major goals for the summer. I decided I was going to try to spend time with my family; I hadn't done that in a long time. I was also going to visit my partners and help them as much as I could. I did not have a clear list of activities because I had to leave as soon as I had all the money. All through the week miracles were coming one by one. However, on June 23, the Lord provided the amount I was missing in a very powerful way. That day, I was on Facebook talking to my friend Adam about what the Lord was doing when I received this message totally unexpected from other friends:

"Hey Tresor, Ted and I wanted to get your phone number because we are probably an answer to your prayer requests! Contact us soon, if you want to reach us"

I immediately called the number my friend had given me on Facebook. My friends told me they had five thousand dollars they wanted to bless me with so I would be able to go to Congo. At this point, the Lord had provided everything I needed. Other friends helped me out the rest of the week I was excited that everything was going well now. I knew now that I was going to go to Congo. It was time now to send emails to my discouraged partners, friends and family to say:

"Hey I am coming, the game is afoot".

Everything was working great and I was happy about that. I had just had a few days to think of what my trip would look like because my departing date was July 9. This was the latest I had ever left for Congo. My plan was to spend at least a month there visiting my partners and spending time with my family and friends.

I booked my flight to arrive on July 11. My travel agent told me I was not going to have my usual flight with Air France through Paris. This time I was going to take a North African airline. I remembered my friends Jace and Shannon telling me they did not receive their luggage for a long time when they travelled to Niger with that same company. I was not really sure I wanted to take that flight, but I did not really have a choice. The only good thing about the deal was that I had a layover in Casablanca, and I was excited by the idea of visiting that beautiful city. I already had my camera ready for this great day of adventure in Casablanca. After all, I deserved a fun time in Casablanca after such a hard summer.

Two days later while I was in the back yard playing with my host family's children, I received a phone call from my travel agent telling me that I would have to fly with another African airline because he could not secure the deal with the other airline. I did not want to take this other one because I had heard stories about late planes and lost luggage every time their name was mentioned. Of course I was reluctant to take the flight but I knew it was my last chance to leave on time so I decided to take it anyway. I packed my bags as fast as I could and made quick arrangements for the time in Congo. The night before I left, my friend Brandon came with a last financial blessing for my trip. Brandon and I talked a little bit before I went to bed. Brandon was telling me to be careful, and he told me stories about lost luggage. That was the last story I heard the night before I left.

Heading to Congo

Monday, July 9, I actually left for the Democratic Republic of Congo. I spent time with my little friends Jada, Striker, Brentley and Onesimus before I left. These children were so attached to me that I had to prepare them for when I would "go bye-bye." I showed my little friends my suitcase and told them I would be leaving them for a while. I left a message with my friend Heather Aldersey who lived in Addis to tell her I was going to be at the airport. We agreed to meet at the airport and maybe share a meal and talk a little bit. My friend Muchengetwa gave me a lift to the airport. I got in the car as my little friends and Lucille waved to me. I knew I was going to miss them, but I was happy to be able to see my family in Congo.

My third journey to Congo started as soon as I sat in Muchengetwa's red car. It was the beginning of an adventure that had a lot of surprises in store. Joy, excitement, apprehension—these were my feelings as I was leaving Joplin. I realized the trip was so unexpected that I did not have time to see Judie, which meant no candies, no Scriptures in envelopes, and probably no journal. I took my black journal with me because I knew I wanted to continue recording stories and personal refection during this trip.

I flew out of Kansas City International Airport. My first flight was from Kansas City to Chicago. I had a lot of time to kill at the Chicago Airport before I boarded the Lufthansa flight to Frankfurt, Germany. I took the opportunity to call a few of my friends to say goodbye and ask for prayers. I talked for a long time with my friend Candy, telling her I was feeling like there was not going to be enough time for something significant to happen in Congo. I was supposed to go to the eastern part of Congo and then work with my friends in Kinshasa on the opposite side of Congo. I had a very short trip, and I felt it was not enough time to allow the significant thing I was waiting for to happen. I was expecting the Lord to give me proof that I needed to continue with the work. I was going with a willing heart and was ready to learn from the Lord. I just did know how it would happen in such a short trip.

On my flight to Frankfurt, I sat next to Adriana who was traveling home for vacation. We talked a lot about art and philosophy as we were flying to Frankfurt. We landed early in the morning in Germany; I had a ten hour layover there. I listened to music the entire time I was at the airport killing time as I waited for my flight to Addis Ababa, the capital of Ethiopia. I could not wait to be home and finally enjoy my family's company. The time finally came for the flight, and I went to find my gate. Unfortunately, we left Germany an hour later than what was scheduled.

On the flight, I was sitting by a German who happened to be going to Congo. He was going to go to Kindu, a city in the center of Congo where I had spent part of my childhood. We talked about Congolese politics and about the region where we were going. As we flew over Germany, he told me about his charitable work with schools around South Africa. He was asking me how he could get a boat while he was in Congo because his partner and he wanted to do a little bit of exploration in Congo. My new friend also wanted some tips about safety in Eastern Congo. I love talking about Congo, and I talked about it all night as we were flying.

We flew over the Nile as the sun was rising. It was great to see the Nile. From up high, it looked like a tiny blue line on brown paper. We landed in Addis Ababa in the middle of the morning. The airport at first looked like Kinshasa with its old planes and old buildings, and in this respect I thought it wasn't much better than Congo. When we arrived at the international terminal, it was a very modern facility, not very different from other airports I had seen in the United States. It was well built, and I was surprised that everything was in order and very clean.

I did not have to wait a long time for my flight to Kinshasa. There were many people at the gate waiting for their flight; many of them were from Congo. I heard a few of them speaking French or other Congolese languages I hadn't heard in a year. As I was sitting quietly trying to recuperate from the day of travel, I turned to my left and noticed a girl sitting by herself behind me. The young lady seemed tired and lost. For some reason I thought she must have been an American.

It was time to board the plane, a steward was giving some instructions I could not understand because of his accent. I walked to the girl and asked her if she heard what the man said. She told me she did not understand either. I asked her if she was from the States and she answered that she was. She was coming from New York.

I was curious to know why a girl from New York would come to Congo, so I asked her what she was going to do in Congo.

"*I am working on a project,*" she answered.

As she was answering, her boarding group was called and she left to go into the plane. I remained there for a while longer until it was time for my boarding group to board the plane. The flight from Addis Ababa was my last stretch home. I was tired and I could not wait to finally land in Kinshasa. We finally landed at the Ndjili Airport after a relatively short flight.

This was the third year in a row that I was home, but this visit had a different taste to it. First, it was the first time I was traveling by myself. Second, I landed at noon instead of the evening like I had always done before. It felt so good to finally be in Kinshasa. There was a fragrance of victory over the long and difficult summer; the airport had not changed since last year. The Presidential Guard, however, had changed uniforms. I saw fewer people in the airport, and there was some kind of order in the airport for once.

The sun was shining but the air was fresh and pleasant, and I was home at last. Though exhausted by almost two days of intense travel, I eagerly expected to see my father at the airport as I had the previous year. My cousin came to pick me up instead. There was noise everywhere at the airport; I think everyone tries to be loud there. The airport in Kinshasa looks nothing like other airports. No one is patient, and everyone has to fight to get his luggage. The travelers have to watch closely so they do not lose their bags to the master thieves at the airport.

While we waited, my cousin (whom I hadn't seen in years) was trying to give me news from home. He informed me that my sisters were waiting in the car outside. As I listened, I was watching to see if my bags were coming out because I did not want anyone to take them. I was so tired. I wanted to be home sleeping in my own bed, and I was already thinking about my mother's cooking. I was getting annoyed because my bag was still not coming.

I looked behind me and saw the girl I had met in Addis Ababa, looking completely lost and tired amidst the chaos of the airport. When I saw her, something inside me told me to go ask her if she needed any help. I sensed it might have been her first time in Congo, and she did not seem to be travelling with anyone.

My cousin continued interrupting my thought process by asking me questions about my school and everything in the United States. We ran into my cousin's friend, Peter, in customs and he also began asking me questions about the United States. He seemed like a pleasant guy, with a big smile on his face. I could tell by his name I might have been related to him. Soon, my cousin began talking to his friend about some personal things, so I decided to walk over to the girl and ask her if there was anything I could do to help her.

Meeting Hannah

The girl told me she was waiting for her luggage. She was traveling alone and was not sure about who was coming to get her at the airport. After she described what her suitcase looked like, I went back in the crowd to try to find her luggage. She seemed nervous so my cousin and I tried to start conversations with her to ease her anxiety. The girl told me that there was a man from the Dikembe Mutombo Foundation at the airport waiting for her. (Dikembe Mutombo is a Congolese NBA star who built a hospital in Kinshasa). She did not know who the man was but he was supposed to pick her up at the airport.

I assumed the girl might have been a doctor or a nurse. I told her that there was a doctor I knew who was coming early in August, and he was going to visit the hospital too. I sent my cousin outside to find the representative of the foundation and tell him that the person he was looking for was inside, still waiting for her luggage. We waited until we were told that there were no more bags in the plane. What Brandon and I had talked about the night before I left Joplin had happened! My bags did not arrive in Kinshasa, and we were not the only ones who did not find their bags. Many others complained their bags did not make it. Peter, my cousin's friend, told us to go file a complaint with the company that handles luggage for the airline.

Peter knew all the shortcuts through the airport, so he led us through the dark and smelly hallways of Kinshasa to beat the crowd to the office. We finally ended up in a tiny office that was very hot and not the cleanest place in the world. It was only when I was helping the girl file her claim that I realized I hadn't asked her name, even though we had been talking for almost an hour now. So, I asked her and she told me her name was Hannah. Hannah spoke neither French nor any Congolese language, so I became her translator. As soon as we finished with all the formalities, we walked out of the office. My cousin met us on our way out of the airport and told us that he did not find anyone from the foundation.

Hannah knew where she was supposed to live during her time in Kinshasa, and she asked me if I could help her find a taxi to get her to her hotel. I offered to take her to her hotel because I knew it was a bad idea to let her go alone with a taxi driver in Kinshasa, and she consented. So we walked to the parking lot where my sisters Rose and Joelle were waiting for me.

While we were walking to the vehicle, my cousin received a phone call from his friend Peter who had also been looking for Hanna's contact. Peter told my cousin that he found the foundation's representative. The man from the foundation came to meet us in the parking lot, but he spoke very little English, so I was again Hannah's translator. I gave Hannah my sister Rose's number, and also exchanged numbers with the young man who came to pick her up. Once we parted, I went back home where my mother was waiting for me. I spent the next few days resting and visiting with my family.

The DMF Project

The next day, my sister and I caught up about life and everything that had happened since the last time we saw each other. My sister told me that she had received a phone call from someone speaking English. Rose did not know who the person was and I could not figure out who it might have been. It could not have been someone from the US, because surely no one knew Rose's number in the USA. I attempted to call the mysterious phone number back but no one picked up the phone, so I called the man from the foundation because I thought that it might have been them calling me. Unfortunately, he did not answer his phone either.

After a long phone-tag game, the mysterious caller called back; it was Hannah, the girl I had met at the airport the day before. Hannah asked me what I was doing until Tuesday, because they needed a translator to help them on their project. She told me that she and her teammates (who had arrived the day before) were filming a video about the foundation. I told her I was willing to help because I knew that promoting the hospital was a noble cause. Hannah asked me to meet her the next day at the Grand Hotel of Kinshasa so she could introduce me to the rest of her team. Although I did not know what to expect, I was excited to help them.

Saturday morning, I went to the hotel to meet Hannah and her friends. I was a little nervous because I did not know what to expect from working with strangers, but I was willing to serve to the best of my ability. When I arrived, I found a crowd waiting at the hotel; they were Dikembe's guests from the States. I then saw Hannah coming in the midst of the crowd, and she took me to the rest of the team. There were three other people on her team: John the sound technician, Steve the cameraman, and Damon the host. I was now part of the crew, and while I was trying my best to get to know everyone, I also had to learn my new job.

I was excited to be part of the media; indeed, it was a childhood dream come true. I was even more excited when Hannah told me what she was expecting from me in the video. It reminded me of what I did with the video about women in war zones, except I had to translate on the field instead of in post production like the other one. I wanted to make my summer count for something and this was a great opportunity. When we loaded the equipment, I met Diffy the driver. Within minutes, we were on our way to a shoe distribution.

I wouldn't have imagined I would be in a media crew when I was leaving Kansas City a few days earlier and yet, here I was! The first thing I did with the team was film a shoe distribution in the downtown area of Kinshasa.

Mr. Mutumbo had a strong entourage and a tight security around him. It was the first time I had ever seen him. I am not a huge basketball fan, so I did not know his accomplishments as a NBA player but I knew him as a man who truly cares for those who are in need. He wanted to do something to change the health situation in Kinshasa, and even the authorities respected him, as evident from a government representative being present at the shoe drop. As the team distributed hundreds of shoes to children,

I found myself admiring what the foundation was doing in the lives of each child who was there, and it was such a blessing to be around.

During the shoe distribution, we interviewed a few children at the school where the event was taking place. Afterward, we went to a restaurant with all the other guests of the foundation. I was just now getting to know my new teammates and finding they were nice people to be around. They made me feel welcomed in the group. Once we finished with lunch, we left the entourage and went on our own to the General Hospital to shoot more footage.

The General Hospital was a reflection of the situation of the entire country. It was in ruins, and offered nothing but memories of a distant place where people once came from all over the region to find quality care. Walking through the hospital reminded me of the time I visited the Kinshasa jail. The conditions at the hospital were not proper for healing. It was a place of desolation.

As I walked through the hospital, I felt it was a place of death and not a path to healing. The people in the hospital were so helpless they begged for money from whoever was passing by. In Congo, the hospital keeps hostage anyone who cannot pay his or her fees. The person is kept at the hospital until the family can pay their bill. Some people had spent a month at the hospital because their families could not afford paying even twenty dollars for their care at the hospital. Because of this policy, despair is a common feature of people's lives at the General Hospital.

Despair also reigned in starving patients who had nothing to eat because their families had not brought them any food. At the General Hospital of Kinshasa, the family is responsible for feeding their relatives at the hospital, which is nothing like in western countries. Some families cook at the hospital, which explains the smell of burnt wood and food inside the hospital.

As I was walking with my new friends, I kept seeing women with their children. The women looked powerless, as they knew there was no medicine in the hospital to treat their children. Yet they were there, believing a miracle could happen. The General Hospital was a very heart-breaking place; its essence is similar to that of a refugee camp. The only difference between the two is that the hospital is not a safe place for those who go there. It was terrible.

We finally came to the children's room after walking through the hospital. We were going to interview the hospital's director as well as a nurse. This particular room was large, and had several beds in it. Hospital patients formed our audience, and the children and their parents were constantly making comments as we were filming. Women were begging me to ask the crew to pay their fees.

While we were interviewing the director and the nurse, I noticed the nurse was closing the door to the room with a lock. I was intrigued, so I asked the patients why they were there. They told me most of the children were well, but they did not have the money to pay their bills, and that is why they were being locked. I realized we were in the hospital "jail" where they kept the children who owed them money. The women were telling me not to forget them as I left the room once we were done filming. This reminded me I was home in Congo, where poverty stained people's faces like tears.

I walked out of that place with a lot on my mind. I knew that the lack of proper care was killing the community in Congo, and I realized the importance of telling people's stories and the value of what I was doing with this new team. We filmed in the hospital's courtyard a bit before leaving. The nurse was impatient because it was his day off. I told him this video could help improve the conditions in the hospital. The people sitting on the grass who listened to Damon speak could not speak for themselves; they needed someone to speak for them. I was glad to be part of that.

Sunday morning we went to a rural area of Kinshasa. We filmed in every site the group visited. It was the furthest east I had been in Kinshasa, because rural areas are the tourist parts of Kinshasa. Indeed, the river is not very far, and it helps people find relaxation from the crowded life of the rest of the city. When we arrived, we shot some footage around the river. The view was beautiful, with the Congo River shining under the sun. After spending some time there, we wrapped the equipment and left for our next destination, a village in Bandundu. This was the first time I had been in that province.

A little ceremony greeted us in the village, for Dikembe was in the middle of the crowd showing how the solar lights that he had given them worked. The people of the village were dancing and celebrating with joy, glad that someone had remembered them. We remained in the village talking to people in the area, and discovered they had neither water nor electricity. A lady told us they hadn't seen electricity in the village for a while, nor did they have clean running water. After we were done filming for the day, we left the village and headed back to Kinshasa. On our way back to town, my head was still processing what I had just seen. I knew those village people were not safe from diseases because of the dirty, contaminated water.

Monday morning was my first visit to the Biamba Marie Hospital. I was impressed when we entered the hospital complex, because Biamba Marie is such a beautiful place. It feels like an oasis of peace in the chaos of Kinshasa. The contrast between the General Hospital we just visited and the Biamba Marie hospital was striking, for there was hope in the Biamba Marie Hospital while the General Hospital was a place of death and despair. We arrived at the hospital in the middle of a ceremony on the parking lot, where many children were being vaccinated against polio. We had a great time meeting people and seeing hundreds of people coming with their children to receive vaccinations for polio and mosquito nets.

The Democratic Republic of Congo is one of the last countries in the world that needs to eradicate polio. I was again translating for the crew and helping with whatever was needed,. At the hospital, I also met my friend Bajana (whom I had not seen for a long time) because her nephew was one of the children being vaccinated. After we finished the interviews outside, we went into the hospital itself. From the first moment, I noticed that Biamba Marie was nothing like other hospitals in Kinshasa. Everything was in order, people were in their rooms, and nurses and doctors were serving them. Being in that hospital gave me hope for the future. We could have other places like that if other Congolese would follow Dikembe's example. On that day I learned that one man can make a difference in the lives of others.

I had the privilege of being present when Damon interviewed Dikembe. He gave of his time and money to build a modern hospital in an area where nobody else would have taken the risk of placing such an expensive facility. Mutombo saw the need and desperation of his people, and he came to their rescue. The Biamba Marie Hospital is a ray of light in the darkness of Kinshasa. I call it a ray because we need more hospitals like that to help the people of DR Congo. When I heard Dikembe speak about the problems of Kinshasa, I could tell he truly cared about the people's lack of proper health care. He is an example for me, and I truly admire that man. Indeed, he is a giant with an angel's heart.

We spent more time at the hospital interviewing a few nurses as well as some doctors. Unlike the other hospitals, the Biamba Marie Hospital staff was there to serve people, and they had all the equipment they needed to do their work. We also visited the Children's Department at the hospital. Again, I found there was no comparison between where we were and the General Hospital we had visited a few days ago. At the Biamba Marie Hospital the quality of care was matched by the heart of the staff. The environment was conducive for healing.

As we continued interviewing people, we met a little boy whose name was Believe. He had malaria, and was becoming anemic because of the severity of his condition. Believe was lying on his bed while his dad was watching him from a chair. We asked Believe's father what was wrong with his child, and he told us the entire story about his son's illness.

Damon asked the father if he was a Christian, and he said he was. Damon and I agreed to pray for the child, that the Lord would heal his disease. After praying for him, I discovered Damon was not only a great guy but was also a brother in Christ, and I rejoiced in my heart about that. After meeting Believe, we visited other parts of the hospital before we left to go back downtown. As we were leaving the hospital, my eyes were glued to these beautiful buildings that really expressed the heart of the man who had such a great vision. The lesson for me was that there is always hope where there is a willing heart.

Tuesday was supposed to be my last day with the crew, since we would be filming for the last time. Anticipating my goodbye, I went early in the morning to their hotel thinking we were going to have a crazy day trying to finish up a few things. Instead, I saw them in the hotel restaurant so I joined them there.

As we were talking, Damon asked me, *"Would you work with us if we stayed until Sunday?"*

I was torn between wanting to go see my little ones at the orphanage (whom I hadn't seen since I arrived) and helping my new friends. Even though I really wanted to go play with the kids, I knew there were far more lives that could be touched with the video. I told Damon I was willing to help as long as it was agreeable with the foundation. Damon told me they wanted to hear more stories from the people in Kinshasa; he asked me if I could help them find these stories. Helene's place was the first one I thought about for such a thing. Since she worked with so many people, I knew that they would find stories among her children.

I told Damon and Hannah that my friend Helene would be a good contact for their project, and we agreed to go visit her orphanage to meet the children and talk about their lives. I called Helene to let her know I was bringing her some visitors, and thankfully, Helene agreed to help with the project. Damon, Hannah and I went to Helene's house in the evening. Shortly after coming to Helene's house, I insisted we visit the new house for street children because I had never seen it. This house was opened as a safe house for former street children. I had met most of the children who were now living there the year before. The ride from Helene's house to the center was not very long. I explained Helene's work to Damon and Hannah while we were driving to the house.

Hannah asked if there were stories of children who had had malaria recently. I remembered that Helene told me there were. She thought there was another story we might have been interested in: a little boy whose leg was burned. Though I did not know a lot of details, we decided to meet the boy. We left the paved road and drove on a dirt road until we arrived at the "Maison De L'espoir" which means "The House of Hope" in French. The house was not yet completed, but the boys were already living there. Helene gave us a quick tour of the house. From our tour, we found the children had a living room downstairs for fellowship, and study rooms and bedrooms upstairs.

I recognized many faces I had seen the year before. Some of the boys came to greet me when they saw me, affectionately calling me their older brother. They had a lot of questions for me about my life in the United States and about my trip to Congo. It was nice to see the smiles on the faces of these children who had endured so much pain in their lives—including my friend Trésor, whom I had met the year before. Once we had finished the tour of the house, we went to the living room where Jean Simon was waiting for us. Everyone gathered in that room to listen to the young man.

Jean Simon

We were given white plastic chairs while Jean Simon was sitting on the floor. We were introduced to Jean Simon Luyindula. Jean Simon could not stretch his left leg. He bore a scar that covered his entire leg, and he had a white band around his knee. My heart was moved with compassion for Jean Simon as soon as I saw him, for I had no idea he was in such distress when Helene told me about him in the car. Jean Simon did not say anything at first; he remained quiet while Helene gave us a brief overview of his story. Jean Simon kept facing the ground with a big and innocent smile. The other boys were teasing him about the fact that he was not saying anything.

Damon told me to ask Jean Simon if he wanted to share his story with us. Jean Simon agreed. Jean Simon was not originally from Kinshasa. Originally, he lived in a village in the western province of Bas Congo with his parents. When Jean Simon was five years old, he and his parents traveled to Kinshasa to sell their agricultural products. While traveling by truck to Kinshasa, they had a wreck and Jean Simon's parents were killed. Jean Simon still remembered seeing his parents' bodies.

"I kept crying," he said.

A rescue team came, took his parents' corpses and put them in a truck, leaving Jean Simon alone and crying on the scene. Another truck driver took pity on Jean Simon, so he put him in his truck and drove him to Kinshasa. Despite the truck driver's compassion, he abandoned Jean Simon as soon as they arrived in Kinshasa.

Jean Simon did not know anyone in Kinshasa. He was moved against his will from a small village in Bas Congo to the capital city of ten million people, and was now at the mercy of the fierce streets of Kinshasa. Jean Simon had to learn the hard life of a street child, as he slept under a shipping container every day. In the morning, he stole everything he needed for his survival and begged every day of his life.

On his best days he made fifty cents to buy some food. In the midst of the horrible circumstances, Jean Simon met a friend who was also living in the street. The friend was older than Jean Simon, so he considered him a younger brother, protecting Jean Simon from the violence of the street. He also fed him and took care of some of his needs. The friend soon found a shelter with an organization that took care of street children, so he took Jean Simon with him to the shelter. When they arrived at the shelter, they discovered that Jean Simon had epilepsy, probably as an aftermath of the accident.

As we sat down listening to him tell these painful memories with courage, I sensed that we were moving to the difficult part because his voice changed, and he gazed down. I was painfully right. Jean Simon soon continued with his story, saying that he was transferred from the shelter in the center of Kinshasa to one in a rural area outside of the city. The organization did this because they wanted to give him more careful attention. One day, Jean Simon was playing with his friends, and they were running around the orphanage with no one there to supervise them. Suddenly, Jean Simon felt dizzy. He started convulsing and fell on a pot of boiling beans during the convulsions. The left side of Jean Simon's body was severely burned.

Helene met Jean Simon and saw him in that condition. She took him in to her new center as soon as it was clean, because it would lower the risk of infection in his wounds. Helene tried to provide health care but the care was not only too expensive but the doctors did not have the skills needed to help him. The look on Jean Simon's face was desperate; he took a deep breath once he was done talking and remained quiet.

After a little break, Damon asked Jean Simon what he wanted to do in life. He told us that he wanted to build houses or make brooms. All of us were laughing because we were expecting him to say something like he wanted to be a doctor or a lawyer, but that was not where Jean Simon's passion was. His heart was in the simple things of life.

Damon turned to me and said, *"This boy is going to walk."*

"I receive it, brother," I replied.

We agreed in the spirit that the Lord was going to perform a miracle in that little life. Damon asked Helene if he could come back and film Jean Simon's day. Helene permitted us to do so.

The next day, we came back to the center to film Jean Simon. Spending time at the center helped us discover Jean Simon for who he is truly is: a sweet little guy who is always ready to serve his friends. We also discovered that Jean Simon had a passion for making brooms. Jean Simon made brooms so that the other children would have no excuse to leave the place dirty. Although he could not walk, he made the brooms for others.

We interviewed him several times that day. During the interviews, he mentioned wanting to go back to school with his peers. He also wanted to be able to go to church to worship God. Jean Simon still remembered playing football (soccer for Americans) with his friends at the shelter. He told me he did not have anything to do during the day and he missed playing so much he made balls for his other friends to use. Then he could watch them play football and feel like he was part of the game. Jean Simon found his joy in helping others do what he could not do. It was a humbling experience to see this orphaned and wounded child use his passion to give to others.

When we finished interviewing him, Jean Simon went to eat. I followed him so we could talk. We had a good conversation, but when I was leaving, Jean Simon had a seizure in front of me.

I did not know what to do. Luckily, he was rescued by the man in charge of the center. I soon realized what the young man was going through, so I prayed for God to open a door to end Jean Simon's suffering. When we were leaving, Damon told me to ask Helene for permission to take Jean Simon to Dikembe's Hospital. Helene granted us permission to take the child to the hospital the next day. As we were leaving the center, I had the feeling that Jean Simon was going to walk very soon. I knew he was going to be healed.

We left early in the morning to take Jean Simon to the hospital. He went through different medical tests while he was at the Biamba Marie Hospital. It did not take long for Jean Simon to become the darling of the Biamba Marie Hospital. After all, he was smiling as always and people loved that about him. Jean Simon was so excited to be in a wheelchair that he wanted one for Christmas. Damon, Hannah and I met with the director of the hospital about Jean Simon's case. He told us that Jean Simon needed a skin graft, but he said that there were two problems: First, he had to find a plastic surgeon to do the surgery; second, he needed money for the surgery. The crew agreed to pay for it and the doctor was given guarantees that the bill would be paid.

The director told us we could take Jean Simon to the hospital the following week. The hospital was going to call Helene and tell her when they would be ready to take the boy in for surgery. We went back where everybody else was and we saw Jean Simon there. He seemed to be feeling better already; his wounds had been thoroughly cleaned for the first time. Jean Simon was still asking who the wheelchair belonged to because he wanted it for Christmas. When we were done with the video work, we sent him back the safe house while we finished other interviews. (The following week, the boy would be in the hospital for more care until he had his surgery). Saturday I took my new friends to Bomo, the girls' safe house, where we met the girls and filmed more.

Sunday morning was our last day together, and was therefore an emotional goodbye. I had had no clue I would meet these people when I was preparing for my trip, but they ended up being the best team with whom I had ever worked.

Back to the Red Soil of Bukavu

After my new friends were gone, I found myself back to my routine. I was running behind schedule, so I decided to fly as soon as I could to Bukavu to visit my partners there. I was not going by myself—indeed, I was traveling with my childhood friend Roland who was going to Bukavu to visit his brother. Because my local team was discouraged, I decided to arrive in Bukavu unannounced so I would surprise everybody. Roland and I flew together to Goma where we spent the night. There, we visited my friends Angi and Marlene and ate dinner with them. The next day we took a boat to Bukavu, by means of Lake Kivu.

The boat we took went too fast to enjoy the travel time, but I still loved it. As soon as we arrived in Bukavu, we went to see Roland's brother. After we were settled, we went to visit my partners in the area. I could not stay very long in Bukavu because I still did not have my luggage. I had been wearing the same clothes for two weeks since I arrived in the city, so I only stayed for four days. I met several people when I was in Bukavu. One of the most encouraging visits I had was when I met the mayor. The mayor of Bukavu has been a long time friend of my family.

He spoke highly of my father, telling me: *"Your father was an honest man—everyone in Bukavu remembers that."* Then he added, *"You can walk with honor in this city."*

I was happy to hear about the impact my dad had left in the lives of the people of Bukavu. The mayor then told me about the struggles of the place where I was born. It was a short trip but I loved every minute of it. I learned a lot from the people I met again.

The Open Wounds of Bideka

In Bukavu I decided to go to Bideka and visit the girls there for some counseling sessions. I went to Bideka early in the morning on a Saturday. I took Bahati, my representative in South Kivu; my childhood friend Roland; and Raphael, a young Congolese man I met the previous year. This was the third year in a row I took the road to Walungu, yet I was still captivated by the beauty of that region. The red soil of Congo still produced a lot of dust as we drove to the mission of Bideka, but the trip to Bideka seemed shorter this time; perhaps because I was now used to going there and was familiar with my surroundings. Despite the fact I knew the region well, I was still very cautious as far as security, because you never know what could happen in the rural areas.

There was a wedding at the church when we arrived in Bideka, so there were a lot more people than usual in the town. The girls were at the house we had been using as a daytime safe place for them. We had been planning to work on the house but still hadn't done anything. There were a few new girls I hadn't met the year before who had joined the group—some of them had been victims of rape. While I was in Bideka, the girls shared their stories. This time was different from previous visits, though, because I now had the confidence of the girls, they trusted me. They even smiled at me; an unusual occurrence for rape victims. They knew they were safe when I was there.

Bahati, Raphael, and I gave Roland a tour of the mission; he was amazed by the beauty of the place. Some of the children who were attending the wedding were following us, wanting us to take pictures of them. After the tour, I went back in the house to talk with the girls. As I listened to them speak, I was torn by their stories. It was so painful to listen to their stories, but these women needed someone to listen to them without treating them as if they were the ones to blame for their condition.

Grace was nineteen when I met her in 2008. She was a devout Christian teenager who enjoyed Sunday school. She never missed church on Sundays. One Sunday while she was attending Sunday school the Interahamwes raided the village. Grace ran as fast as she could, unfortunately, she and three other girls were caught by the militia. She was looking down, her lips were shaking as she was telling me these painful parts of her past.

She told me with a trembling voice, *"They circled us, and raped us. They did horrible things to us. They beat us with an extreme violence, and tied our hands. I was raped by nine men. It hurt, and my pain would not go away."*

The militiamen took her to the mountains where she was made a sex slave; she was mistreated daily.

With tears in her eyes, she said, *"We were nothing more than animals in the eyes of the Interahamwes we were mere objects. The men did whatever they wanted to us, and always guarded us closely so that we would not run away."*

One day the Interahamwes sent her and other women to the creek without any guard. She took her courage and fled from the Interahamwes camp. Grace returned to her village but she was mocked by other members of the community because she was raped. Grace has never had a chance to be tested for HIV. She lives with fear because she thinks that she has HIV. She also has a son who is not accepted by the community because he was born from a rape.

Grace's story is one of the many that need to be heard. Her life is one of the many that needs to be changed. Before I left, I gave the girls some money to take care of their needs. It was very little but they were very thankful for it. After taking a few pictures, we started getting ready to leave Bideka. I saw one of the girls carrying a heavy sack, probably headed to the market; because women in Eastern Congo put what they will sell in a sack tied around their head, carrying it for miles before they get to the market. I felt powerless and told myself that someday none of my girls will have to do that work anymore.

Returning to Kinshasa

I left Bukavu Sunday with the feeling that I could have done more if I stayed longer, but time was against me. I ended up on an extremely slow boat as I left Bukavu. We finally arrived in Goma after five hours of travel. Marie Noelle was coming to get me but I had never seen her. Marie Noel worked with victims of sexual violence in Goma. We didn't have much time to talk, though, because she had to get me to the airport.

I was late for my flight, but luckily, the plane was still there when we arrived. I rushed through the lines, running as fast as I could. I made it to my flight and, two hours later, I was back in Kinshasa. My mind was full of vision for Bukavu but at the same time, I was trying to process everything I had heard. I returned to Kinshasa just in time to get back to my unfinished business: Jean Simon's situation.

God at Work

When I arrived in Kinshasa my friend Carrie told me her parents were on their way, since we agreed that they would visit for my mother's birthday. My friend Christian and I showed them to my parents' house. We did not have time to see the children at the orphanage because Carrie's parents had to go to Tanzania. We did talk about Congo, and everything we were trying to accomplish. I told them about my adventure with Hannah and Damon at the beginning of the summer. As we were eating plantains and chicken they listened carefully to the story I was telling them, I also mentioned what happened to Jean Simon. After dinner, we fellowshipped at the house until it was late.

The following weeks were a mixture of meetings and reconnections with my partners. I went to visit the work of Vorsi Congo. Then I followed up with Helene on the work we had done. I visited the girls again at BOMO and went to see the clothes they bought with the money Damon had given them when he was there. The girls were so excited about having new clothes and shoes to wear. They kept smiling as we took pictures of them and their gifts. I spent a lot of time with Helene talking about what happened with Jean Simon. Helene told me the day when I called her she had been praying God would open a door for Jean Simon to be able to walk again. She told me I was really an answer to their prayers. I was glad the Lord used me in helping this child regain the use of his legs.

God Answered Jean Simon's Prayer

Helene called me to tell me I needed to go to the Biamba Marie Hospital. She said that there was something I needed to see there. I did not know whether she was expressing her discontent at the fact Jean Simon had been there for a while or something else had happened. The people at the gate recognized me from the time when I came with the team earlier in my trip, so even though it was not time to visit, they were kind enough to let me see Jean Simon. They even sent someone to guide me to Jean Simon's room. My friend, Christian, was amazed to see such a nice place in Kinshasa. Many of the nurses remembered me from when I came before, and they came to say hello and to ask if I had any news from the team. Jean Simon was asleep when I arrived in his room.

As soon as I arrived, I was told the good news: Jean Simon had had a surgery on his leg. Helene told me that an American doctor came in to do the surgery. The nurse was with us, and he was checking on Jean Simon while he was asleep. I asked the nurse if he knew who did the surgery. He told me that he could not remember but the man was an American doctor. He added that the doctor's last name was difficult to pronounce.

"Does his daughter work at the Embassy?" I asked curiously.

"Yes, I think so but I am not sure." He replied.

It was clear to me that he was talking about Dr. Joe, Carrie's father, whom I had met two weeks before.

The noise of our conversation woke Jean Simon from his deep sleep. Jean Simon slowly opened his eyes. He looked at me as if he did not recognize me, then he had the sweetest smile on his face. My heart was full of joy when I saw the young man in his bed. I had flashbacks of the days we were filming him. I remembered how bad his wound was before, and how he could hardly walk. I recalled Damon telling me the first night we met Jean Simon: *"This boy will walk."*

I was happy. Jean Simon almost jumped out of his bed when he realized that I was the one standing in front of him.

"Is that really you?" he shouted.

Jean Simon gave a long hug while his roommate, a pastor, was staring at us. Jean Simon began to tell me stories of his surgery. He told me that the doctors gave him something that made him forget most of what happened. Everyone at the Biamba Marie Hospital knew Jean Simon—he always told hilarious jokes. Jean Simon's presence brightened everybody's day in the surgery department.

"This child can make anyone laugh," his nurse said.

The little orphan boy became the darling of the Biamba Marie Hospital. I was so happy to see the care Jean Simon received at the hospital. I went back home after taking a few pictures to send to Damon. On my way back home, I could not stop thinking that losing my luggage was the best thing that had happened to me because Jean Simon was going to walk as an indirect result. A month before, I thought that my summer was lost but now it turned into a miracle for a child. I sent Carrie a text message asking her if her dad had done surgery at the hospital.

"Yes, He did. On the boy you took there. We are really a connected family."

God had set things in motion a long time ago to answer a child's prayer. Jean Simon was crying for help and God heard him, so He sent a group of people who did not know each other to come to his rescue. I couldn't keep from smiling when I thought that Jean Simon wanted to have a wheelchair for Christmas but was now going to walk. God hears the prayers of His children.

Miracle: Jean Simon Walks!!!

Two weeks after Jean Simon had his surgery, I returned to Joplin to start my final year in college. I was two weeks late for classes, and I never found my luggage. Although I left Joplin with one hundred pounds of luggage, I returned with only my school bag. I was back to the calm little town of Joplin working toward the completion of my college career. I had my own plans when the summer started, but the Lord turned my trip into a powerful testimony for everyone involved.

A month after I left Kinshasa, Helene sent me an email that made me jump from my chair and shout praises to heaven. The email read:

"My heart is celebrating as I write to you. Jean Simon is walking! And no one needs to help him. He does not have crutches."

What an epilogue for my years of research in Congo to have Jean Simon walking. The Lord taught me what I needed to know after three years of trying to understand the problems of Congo—there is hope because He is in control, and He knows the timing.

He has the resources and as soon as He gives permission, the work will be successful no matter what the world thinks. As I forwarded the email to everyone, I was happy that my luggage was lost because I saw how everything was so well lined up for that to happen. Jean Simon's story is a story that will mark my life forever, and I am blessed to have been part of his healing.

Epilogue:

I embarked on a journey to bring change to the world three years ago. The first stop is Congo, and I know that the rest of the world is coming next. I started my journey thinking things were going to go easy but I realized the world is not a safe place. You get hurt in many ways. I found out that even when you fall, you need to stand up and persevere in your work. When I sat in Judie's office before my first trip, I had no idea this was the beginning of a journey that would lead to publishing this book. I did not know that I was going to write a book the day I met the lady in yellow at Kidodobo.

I have realized through my journey that even in the midst of horror, there is hope, as long as there are people willing to devote themselves to change the world. Peace and reconciliation are possible, but they only happen when people decide to forgive each other with a sincere and honest heart. The victims will actually find peace in forgiving their perpetrator. I am not saying they will not have to pay for their actions. Everyone who has committed these horrible crimes will have to pay for what they have done. However, the first lesson from my trips is that healing will come only when true forgiveness is extended. This is the hardest part, but I have noticed that those who have forgiven their abusers were able to be more successful in life.

How we can help this situation? The first thing we can do is be advocates for the victims. We need to proclaim that there is hope for them and that we care in word and, more importantly, in deeds. We need a commitment from humanity to not let things like what is happening in the Democratic Republic of Congo happen anywhere else, even though, unfortunately, it is now happening in other parts of the world. Rape victims, child soldiers, street children, AIDS orphans, and child prostitutes deserve our help. They deserve our care as fellow human beings.

I tried my best in this book to expose the different aspects of the crisis in Congo. You have read these stories—perhaps you have shed a few tears, but all this will be meaningless if we do not take action to change these situations. There are no small things you can do to effect change, because anything done with a sincere heart can change the world. I know it has hurt you to read some of the pages of this book. Maybe you are angry that these things happen in the world today. However, if we do not turn our anger and pain into tangible action, the purpose of writing this book is completely defeated.

There are many ways you can get involved in bringing a positive change in our world. You can get involved in the organization I started. Go to our website and learn how we are planning on changing lives in post-conflict countries all over the world, and in Congo in particular. Go to www.littlethingsgreatlove.com to learn more about our work. This is just one way you can get involved in changing things. There are many other organizations that work in the same field as well. I did not write this book to push the agenda of my organization, I do not care if you give money to someone else or if you volunteer for some other organization but by all means DO something to help change this situation. We cannot sit back and let this happen anymore.

It is a shame that during King Leopold's time the world did not notice an estimated one million people died in Congo from all sorts of atrocities. Today, more than five million people have died, and we have barely noticed. I do not know about you, but these kinds of things make me angry and cause me to want to take action in order to make this world a better place.

Now that you have heard about these things, ignorance can no longer be your hiding place and an excuse to not take any action. We need to stand up and do something. Even the smallest thing when it is done in love means a lot to the people who receive it. I have witnessed the power of small things over and over. The people who have agreed to share their stories in this book decided to share their shame, humiliation and suffering because they knew that it would help make the world a better place. I remember the glow of fear in their eyes, the tears and their grave voices when they told their stories. We need to bring an end to these issues so that what they did will not be meaningless. War victims are people who deserve our love, attention, and help.

Those of us who have seen them and the desperation in which they live know it is time to do something tangible. I will never forget that day in 2006 when the lady in yellow grabbed my hand and told me, "Tell my story." This is a promise I intend to fulfill. I hope that you are going to join me in this effort. I have hope because I already see people rising up and speaking up for the poor and the oppressed, but we need more people to speak up against these issues. Rape victims, street children, AIDS orphans, child prostitutes and child soldiers have opened up their hearts to you and told you their story. They are crying out for help. So, please extend a helping hand and write a new page in their lives. Let's work together in making the world a better place!

Slum in Kinshasa

Mother and daughter praying

Children in Bukavu

Blaise

I joined a group called "local defense" in 2004. We were told that we would receive money if we joined them. They said that they would give $100(US) to each person who would join the armed group. My parents are really poor and they could not feed us. I thought that it was a chance for me to take care of myself and my family so I joined them. I know now that it was a mistake.

I was trained to use guns and knives at a camp. They gave us uniforms and told us that we would be deployed in Kalehe. We were posted there for two months when the Mai-Mai attacked us and looted all we had. We tried to fight them back but they were stronger and captured us. They tortured and beat us harshly. When the opportunity came we fled to go back home but we ended up here in Kavumu. The police have been harassing us because we are former child soldiers. All I want is to be a carpenter and have a new chance in life. (Blaise, Former Child soldier)

Woman in Kinshasa

Appendix A

Child Soldiers: Heroes or Losers

Child soldiers are the sad reality of most civil wars in the world. There are an estimated 250,000 children under the age of 18 fighting in conflicts all over the world. Sometimes they are as young as seven when they are either abducted or lured into the militia. They usually have to go through a ritual of acceptance that includes murder or rape. Most of them have killed their own relatives.

Militias like having child soldiers because of their obedience and unawareness of the danger around them. These children are used for various jobs like carrying the equipment, fighting, and marketing girls as sex slaves for adult soldiers. Some of the militias believe that children have magical powers and that their presence helps them become invincible. These children are usually used as the first line in a battle.

Estimates of the number of child soldiers in the Democratic Republic of Congo are as high as 30,000. Some estimates state that 10,000 of them have been demobilized from militias. For those who are still in the militias, the challenge is escape. Those who have fled or have been demobilized must face the rejection and the challenge of being re-inserted into their communities. The conflict in DR Congo is not over and reports note new abductions in the eastern and northeastern regions of the country. The challenge is to bring hope to those who are no longer soldiers, to free those who are still soldiers, and to prevent the militias from kidnapping more children.

The term used for these children is "Kadogo." This Swahili word means "little one." Today there is a distinct definition of child soldiers, namely: "children associated with armed groups." The first time these children were seen was during the rebellion of 1996, although I remember my cousin, in the presidential guard during Mobutu's time, saying he was taken to join the army when he was twelve.

During the war of 1996, an army of children marched from the hills of Eastern Congo to the capital city of Kinshasa. They were welcomed in every city with shouts of praises and celebrations. They were called the Kadogos.

From Kinshasa (where I was living during the rebellion against Mobutu), I watched the child soldiers take city after city. I still remember a commander being interviewed on a French station saying the child soldiers were very efficient because they did not have the cares that adult soldiers had. My friend's dad was in the army, and the stories he told us about what was happening at the frontline usually including the capture of "kadogos". I still vividly remember him saying: *"You have no idea of how hard it was to kill these children"*. But it was war and these children were the enemy.

In 1997, the army of children reached the capital city of Kinshasa. May 17, 1997, a day that made history, was the day Mobutu was overthrown after thirty-two years in power. He fled the city, leaving Kinshasa at the mercy of the "kadogos". They were a strange sight for the population—some of them just a little taller than the gun they were carrying.

My mother, who was courageous enough to go to the market that day, told us when she returned home: "When the commanders are not there, they play football like any other child but when the adults are back they become aggressive with people".

The child soldiers so infested Kinshasa that "kadogo" became a common nickname in the city. Even during a military parade I remember the presenter praising a child for being the head of his company. But no one really knew what kind of struggle these child soldiers were facing in their heads. Although they had defeated Mobutu in one war, they were fighting another war, one between the child they really were and the soldier they were made to become.

Their Stories

Child soldiers have always had a special place in my heart because of the kind of horror they go through and what they are forced to do. The Kadogos came from eastern Congo where I was born, each time I saw one of them, I remembered that I could have been one of them. These children who have been promised glory and fame are the losers of the war in Congo. Child soldiers are victims and victimizers in the conflict. They have been forced to do all sorts of things. In my travels in DR Congo, I met some of them who shared their stories with me. The longest one is Murhula's story. I met him in 2007 and he wrote several pages that reveal his experience in the militia. The others are boys that I met in another area of the East. Their names have been changed to protect their identities. These stories should invite us to do more so that no child in this world is forced to fight a war.

Soldier in the frontline

John

I was kidnapped when I was eleven. I remained with the militia for a year and a half. I remember that the news came to my village that the war was coming again. I remember one day people were running everywhere, they were shooting everywhere. I had no choice but run as well. I fled to Nyatshibamba. There were eight more boys with me. All of us were running away because we did not want them to take us and make us fight for them. We found a hiding place but we were in very difficult conditions. They were shooting every day; it never ended. We were sleeping in conditions that even animals wouldn't stand.

One day, we thought that the battle was over and there was no more danger. We started walking back home. We were close to a creek. The rebels were on the bridge; they saw us and captured us. They took us to Walungu. They told us there that we were now fighters and we were incorporated into their armed group. They took us to fight many battles. I did things that were terrible, but I had no choice. At last, we were defeated by the government troops. They also captured us because they considered us as enemies. We explained to the officers that we were captured and forced to fight with the militia. The officers believed us. They took us to Bukavu and we were demobilized. Since then I live with fear. I am not at peace because of all the things I have done. Years have passed but nothing changes in my life. I am trying to find hope and start

Soldiers in Walungu

They took me from my house. I was with other friends. They made us follow them to the mountains. We had to walk through the bushes. There were thorns everywhere that cut my skin. I was a slave for the commander. I had to do everything he wanted. I do not know my parents anymore. I don't know anything. I want to learn and be able to be somebody some day.

They took me to a military camp and they trained me there. Our instructor was a Rwandese soldier. He told us we would become bodyguards for the commander. We were frightened. The adult soldiers burned our clothes and gave us military clothes to wear.

Life is really hard in the camp. They fed us, but we were beaten all the time. I could not understand what was happening to me. I still do not understand what happened. When I would tell them I was sick, the only answer they had was to beat me up. They forced us to roll ourselves in the mud. I got my chance to escape and I did (Karl, former child soldier)

Murhula

First of all I want to say something to my brothers who have been child soldiers. I am so thankful to God Almighty because many of those who were in the army never saw their families. Some never had a chance to leave the army. Others died and never saw their families. But I was fortunate enough to see my family again. We became child soldiers blindly. Now that we are out of this life, we should try to make our life back. I know that we have all been exposed to bad things—we have been with girls, we have taken drugs.... I pray that all of us are going to be out of this life very soon.

About work in the camp, I can only say that it is not work. You get paid to work, but we were only exploited in that place. I wish I had kept studying because the army is no place for children to excel in that way. I would love to have an education instead of being a child soldier. We all know that soldiers used to confiscate students' cards and tear them up because they envied the fact that those students could go to school. The camp was a place where I learned to steal things, take drugs and drink alcohol. I did so many bad things that I regret today.

During my time in the army, I fought many battles. Some of the places I fought are Burhuza, where I fought the Rwandan army. I fought in Mashango Burhale against the Interahamwes. I also fought battles at Kankinda, Mulamba, Ntondo, Burhindy and Tubimbi—let me tell you, it was not an easy task. I am thankful to God that in all these wars, I returned alive.

Guarding the camp at night was the hardest task for us child soldiers. We had to stand on our feet all night until daylight. We either walked around all night or would be seriously punished. It is no joke to stay up all night waiting for the enemy to come.

Our enemies, the Interahamwes, were always trying to come get us. We also had to patrol the surrounding villages. Our task was to collect information and send it to the camp. If we saw an enemy, we would shoot in the air so that everyone at the camp would come to help us fight the enemy. We didn't have the right to sleep. The only exception was that at midnight everyone had to take a ten minute break. I belonged to a traditional militia tied to the Bashi tribe. The name of that army was "Mundundu 40". The reason why we had to stop for ten minutes was based on a traditional belief that says; "All evil spirits and all demons walk around at midnight. That is why nobody is allowed to walk around or he would be severely punished".

Mornings were not easy times for us. We were guards at night and we had to train in the morning. Our commanders would train us to make sure we remembered everything we were taught in case we had to go fight that day. Day after day they reminded us that we had to fight so we did not forget the reason why we were there. After that we would be tested on our knowledge. We had a little time to rest; especially if you were chosen to go guard the commander, you did not have a chance to rest for the entire day.

Those who stayed in the camp could wash their clothes and do other chores that were needed for the camp that day. In the evening we would gather around the pole and recite incantations for two hours. After the incantations we had another training session. Afterwards, we had to start getting ready to guard for the night. This is why the militia is such a terrible place. We didn't study anything. All we learned was to steal and violate the rights of others. There was no respect for our lives. There was no interest in our growth. Militia life is nothing but a curse and bad luck. After going through all that, I pray that the Lord lead me to a job that is going to make me useful in this world. I would love to have an impact on my family and on my community. I am not the only one who went in the army looking for money and a better life. We were all blinded.

I lured myself into thinking there would be good life for me in the army. I was afraid my dad would punish me, and I decided to run to the militia. I thought I would be taken care of. I was a fool. Life in the militia is like being in hell. I should have thought before I acted. I was running away from misery and I got more than what I was trying to escape.

When I arrived at the camp, I felt happy because they were smiling and surprised to see a boy who went to school join them. The day we started training was the worst day of my life. I thought we were just children but I realized none of the promises they told us were going to become a reality. It was a painful experience. I wanted to go back home but I knew they would kill me if I tried to run away. If only my home was closer, I would have tried.

When you are a child soldier, you have no say. They do whatever they want to you and you have nowhere to complain. Even a slave has more value than a child soldier. The adults would come and insult us whenever they wanted. They treated us like prisoners. We were beaten all the time to the point I was dreaming about home and my family every day. I wished I could go back to them but it was impossible because we were guarded like prisoners. In the morning they would wake up and be sent to the training. We were taught incantations and whoever could not remember was beaten even worse than a snake.

Each passing day got longer. It went from bad to worse. Those who had a chance to run away did so and they went back home. As for me, I missed the opportunity to run away so I was stuck in this life of a militiaman.

There were only two of us who finished the training: my friend Ombeni and I. We arrived on a Saturday, I remember, and we spent a month being harshly trained. There were three other children with us, but they succeeded in escaping the camp. After training we joined an armed group, and I remained in Lurhala for three months. From there I was sent to a hill called Mumbiri; I had a lot of friends there. I was happy to be around them. I was then sent to my father's village: Mushinga. My grandparents still live there. I became good friends with the other children there. We looked after each other like we were children from the same mother.

I didn't find any satisfaction in the militia. Some of the other children seemed to enjoy that life sometimes. They had forgotten everything their parents taught them. They only knew what the commanders told us. How to steal from the peasants, rape women, and take drugs–that is all they knew. The commanders told us that the only interest of this work is to be respected and have all we want but I know the only way child soldiers do that is by violating the rights of others.

When I was in Mushinga, I had a commander who feared God. He would tell all his bodyguards to go with him to church on Sunday. I also tried to remain faithful to God while I was in the militia. I talked to my friends about God but they did not like it. But I was happy that we had to go to church for an opportunity to worship.

I believe that I ceased to be a child the day I went to fight for the first time. Because at that point I knew I could take another life. I knew I had to make a decision between me and them. There was no more right or wrong in my mind.

We went everywhere chasing and fighting the Rwandese, our enemies. My life was in danger every day. That first battle took place in Burhale where we were fighting the Rwandese (Interahamwes). It was a Friday. We fought for nine hours straight, from 5:00 a.m. to 2:00 p.m. We always fought the Hutus. Day and night we patrolled to make sure they would not come back. My life was always in danger because they could attack us at any time. And as I guarded the camp, I had to be careful in case they would choose to attack that night.

I remember one day we went to fight, and I was praying in my heart that God was going to protect me. I would have been dead if it wasn't for him. That day we went from the camp of Mushinga to fight the Interahamwes. On our way to the battle we were attacked by surprise. When that happened, our commander ran and left us there. When he was running away, he left his radio. I saw that and started wondering what would happen if we ran out of bullets. There was no one to ask for reinforcements.

In the chaos, I took the radio from another child soldier who could not use it, and we started running together. Then my friends took another route while I chose to follow the route my commander took when he left us. I didn't know that the Interahamwe had already taken that route.

I was surrounded. I was so afraid that I was going to die that day. I kept running through the trees trying to climb the hill, but the Interahamwes had already conquered the top of the hill. There weren't any of my friends there. I was surrounded by Interahamwes. I looked back and forth, to my left and to my right, but none of my friends were there. I was wondering where I was going to run. There seemed to be no place to go. I was praying in my heart: "My Lord, I am in your hands. I don't have any brothers. I don't have any friend. I have no one else than you, Lord. Please save me."

I felt fear growing in my heart. I was telling myself death was on its way to get me. All of a sudden I felt strong again, and I put the radio in my pocket. I held my gun tight and started firing at them. They were firing back at me but I was running as fast as I could. I could hear them scream: "Get him! He can't escape us… Get the child!"

I was holding two guns: mine and my friend's who died during that battle. I had my gun on my back and was using my friend's to fight. I fought that day until there were fewer of them. I saw how many there were against me, and I knew I had to escape.

I saw the fight was losing intensity. I took advantage of the time they were taking to reorganize themselves and fled. I knew they would get me and keep me hostage and if that happened, death was better. I started running as fast as I could to climb another hill. I turned back and fired at them as they were firing back at me. Finally, I saw on top of the hill that some of my friends were coming to my rescue. Ten of them came to help me and the other ones kept fighting the Interahamwes. I thanked God that day because I was left alone fighting for more than two hours against a multitude of people and He kept me alive.

I saw so many bad things when I was in the militia. We were considered animals. We were made to be criminals and murderers.

They made us evil, and we could not tell the difference between good and evil anymore. Everyone thinks we are murderers and, therefore, we deserve death. We end up becoming thieves and some are burned alive in the streets of Bukavu.

Some of us were forced to rape women. I think those carry a curse with them for the rest of their lives. They have raped women who were their mother's age and girls who were their sister's age. I wish they would respect the rights of these women and girls the way they would want people to respect their own mothers and sisters, but they did not have a choice. Being a child soldier is a curse! It only leads to death.

I was not pleased with the way my life was going at that time. I started thinking about my parents. I realized the commanders were lying to me. I was thinking about a way to escape the camp and go back home. I found the occasion when I was guarding the camp. The commander was gone that day, and I told my friends I was going to buy alcohol at the local market. The rule was to always walk in a group. I just told my friends they could rest and there was no danger since I knew they were tired from being up all night, and the commander was not there to enforce the rule.

I gave them my gun, and one of my companions asked me, "Why don't you take your gun with you?"

I told him I wanted to have my hands free to carry the drinks for the five of them. When I walked past the camp and I was sure they could not see me anymore, I started running. I was running as fast I could. I got rid of my military uniform and went on the main road. A truck driver stopped to give me a lift, and he dropped me in a village. I started walking when all of a sudden I met a patrol from our militia.

Their commander looked at me and recognized I was a soldier. He asked me what I was doing there so far from my camp. I told him my commander sent me to bring clothes to his wife who was in a village around there. I saw that he had a radio in his hand. I was terrified he would call my commander and ask about this. I started praying he would not do that. I did not have any clothes with me when I claimed I was going to give them to my commander's wife.

He finally told me to go on but to get back early because we had operations coming up. I kept walking without looking back. When I couldn't see any soldier, I took another road. I walked until I was getting close to home. I saw a vehicle was about to leave going to Mugogo. I asked the driver if I could jump in and he agreed. When we arrived at the market in Mugogo, I saw my mother. She was selling at the market. I went and greeted her. She seemed frightened so there was not that much reaction when we saw each other.

I started walking to Bideka. When I arrived in the center of the village, I met child soldiers coming from the camp on the mountain not very far from where I lived. They told me I was a soldier and they would take me back to the camp with them. They knew me because I was part of their group after my training. They were from Lurhala. I tried to resist, but I knew I would be in great trouble if I did not obey them. After hesitating, they let me go home. I went to my friend Barhonyi's place.

I talked with his parents telling them how life was in the camp. I told them that I was sorry for all the things I had done. They gave me some food to eat. Barhonyi walked me back—he left me half way, and I walked the rest of the way by myself. As I was walking I saw the child soldiers who stopped me earlier. They were back. They arrested me and took me to their camp. This happened on a Saturday. I stayed there for a week, but because they could not make contact with my commander, they let me go. It was Sunday of the following week.

I left that camp running as fast as I could. I was going through the bush, running between trees. I did not want them to change their minds and come get me again. I finally arrived in our neighborhood but did not want to spend the night at home for fear they would come look for me. My father told me to go hide in Bukavu, and my older brother went with me. I was supposed to spend only a week there but I became ill. I stayed in Bukavu for two months while I was healing. When I came back to Bideka, the soldiers came to our house again saying that I had to go back to the militia.

My father mustered up his courage and told them: "My son just escaped from death and you want him to go back? He is not going with you."

My father gave the soldiers twenty US dollars and then they left. They came back a week later, and this time my father gave them a goat so they would leave me alone. After that, they never came back to look for me. I stayed at home with my family while I was healing.

My father talked to me about God a lot and how much he loves me. We read scripture, and I asked my family for forgiveness. I decided to serve God and be a good child to my parents. I hope parents who have children that have been in the militia will still love them. These children are still their children. It is sad to see that parents would sometimes reject their children because they had been child soldiers. Hating child soldiers is not the solution to the problem.

When I came back home, I realized the militia is really a curse. Before I became a child soldier, I had a lot of friends. When I became a child soldier, my friends started wondering, "How come Murhula became a child soldier? He has always been a good boy." I remember a few people sent me letters when I was in the militia telling me to come back home and I refused. I was blinded; I did not know what I was doing.

When I came back, I did not have any friends. There were some of my old friends who would run away from me. Some of them would pass me on the street and ignore my presence. They would not even extend a greeting to me. I would find myself begging them: "Brothers, do you not remember me? How can you pass by me without even saying 'Hello' to me?"

I would try to do anything to show that I was happy to be back and to see them again. Most of them would just say a little "Hello" and leave me. I realized that almost everyone was afraid of me. But I worked hard and changed. Most of my friends who were child soldiers like me are not as fortunate. They still have no friends.

Some of my neighbors were nice to me. They welcomed me like you would welcome anyone who comes back from a journey. But most of them did not have any compassion toward child soldiers. I am sure some of them wanted me to die in the militia, and they did not have a tear for me. Others feared me because they believed child soldiers bring evil spirits with them. Today, I feel I have made peace with my village, but many of those who went through the same things as me do not have the same chance.

Sometimes I wonder if I learned anything from the militia. I don't think I learned anything there—it is a life without education, a life of misery. I know I was blinded; I started loving things like stealing, alcohol, insults, sexual relations, all kinds of evil. I now regret all these things I have done under the influence of my commanders. I enjoy not having to steal to eat. I am glad there are people who care about me and give me advice because usually, no one wants the best for children in the militia.

I am also glad my teachers welcomed me like any other child. They thought of me like everyone else. They did not persecute me because I was a child soldier. The only times I am tempted to think about going back to the militia is when I don't even have fifty cents to get food.

If I was hungry in the militia, I would steal from the peasants or violate their rights so they would pay me. But I would not return to the militia for anything. I saw all kind of things in the militia. Some of the children would go and put up road blocks and force people to give them money. Some others would go to the village to kidnap young girls to go wash their clothes. I had a good friend named Birindwa. I often wonder what he became.

Dear reader, what you just read is the story of Murhula Bishiakabalya. I believe you have found out who I am, who I was and who I long to be. Please read this closely so that no other child will blindly fall into the mistake I made as a child. I recommend that all of us put our trust in God. I also recommend to the parents to love their children who have fallen in the traps of the militias. I wish you a long and better life with all the luck possible.

Appendix B:

Sexual Violence: the plague of eastern Congo.

Sexual violence is the plague of the Democratic Republic of Congo. Hundreds of thousands of women have been and are being brutally gang raped by those fighting a war no one understands. It is hard to know why a human being would do such things. Many women report being raped by multiple men. I have heard stories of women who have been raped by sixteen or twenty men. Today, rape is not used just for mere sexuality - it is not just a byproduct of war. It is in fact a weapon. It is a barbaric act with the intent of creating fear in the population.

Rapes in Eastern Congo are not just isolated cases. They are systematically conducted. The goal is to dehumanize the victim. Sexual violence humiliates the woman, who is the base of the family. She is the one who cares for the children; she is the guardian of the household stability. In many cases in DR Congo, she is the bread winner. Destroying women's humanity and worth therefore breaks stability in families and societies. It brings shame to the entire community. The perpetrators seek to destroy that stability in order to break the resistance to their power. Once the community is filled with fear, the militias can make the people of the community do whatever they want.

Women in Eastern Congo have seen their honor stripped away from them. I visited Bukavu for the first time in 2006. People were still marked by what happened in June 2004. They told me how the rebels, led by Colonel Jules Mutebutsi, went from house to house raping each woman they found. They did not have an age limit; it was reported that they went from 3 year-olds to 70 year-olds. A friend told me that the rebels would go from house to house.

"They would ask for cell phones and girls. When they found a woman in a house, they would rape her right there," she told me.

"They had no respect for ages. They would rape a mother and force her husband and children to watch" she added.

It is hard to believe but fathers have been forced to rape their own daughters, and brothers their own sisters. In some cases, some women have been raped in public places while the violators forced the entire village to watch. Is there a worse way to destroy a life? Is there a more horrid manifestation of evil in the heart?

As if that is not enough pain, the women are also forced to carry everything the militias have looted from their village. Tied like slaves, they are forced to follow militiamen to their hiding place where the women are then turned into sex slaves. Some women report having been put in a cage or tied up in the middle of the camp, where any man who wanted to could rape them whenever he wanted. The women are also forced to be maids for their abusers and forced to carry their abusers' equipments when the men go to battle. They have to experience the bitterness of giving birth to a child that looks like the man who destroyed their lives. That is, when they can recall who the father was.

Those who succeed in escaping have to face the rejection of their community. They lose their husband, and people make fun of them because they have been raped. Their children are also rejected by the community for being born out of rape. On top of that these women develop fistula. This abnormality is a direct result of instances when militiamen use knives, sticks and sometimes shoot bullets into the vagina when they are raping women. Let's not forget AIDS and all the sexually transmissible diseases that militiamen carry with them. Life loses its meaning when all you have to live for is rejection and trauma, and when all the dignity you have left is stripped away from you.

Their Stories

During my travels in Eastern Congo, I collected stories of women who had been victims of sexual violence. I compiled them in my journal. I feel that it is my duty as one who has heard these stories to share them. I tell these stories not for the sake of just raising awareness but to fulfill a promise to the victims. I promised them to be a voice for them. The names used in these testimonies are not the actual names of the girls. I wanted to protect their identity and keep them safe. Some of the stories are not very detailed. The girls were still under intense trauma and some of them could not say more than a paragraph. I decided to place them here because they deserve to be heard. My hope is that these stories will help you realize the cruelty of what has happened and is still happening to thousands of women in DR Congo as you read this. Please do not keep these stories to yourself; share them and call people to action. Together we need to put an end to these barbaric and degrading practices.

Aline

I am an orphan. My parents are dead. Christine is my friend; I spent some of my days at her house. She is just like a sister to me. Her parents always treated me well. They loved me as their own child. One evening, I was at their house for supper. When we finished eating, I felt the need to go to the bathroom. Because it was dark outside, I asked Christine's sister to come walk with me to the outhouse. While I was in there, I heard noise coming from the house; it sounded like someone was breaking the door. I tried to call the sister's name but she was not answering. I got out and walked to the house in the dark. I noticed the door seemed to have been broken with an axe.

"Who opened the door?" I shouted. There was no answer. I walked into the house. I saw there were a lot of people in the house. They had put the family in one corner. They were asking Christine's sister to give them money. He was a farmer so they assumed he had a lot of money with him. All of them were wearing masks; they talked to each other in Kinyarwanda. They had flashlights, and they started looking for what they wanted. They were taking everything the family had. They looted everything, even the goats outside. They came back and started beating the father to the point his nose was bleeding.

One of them pointed at me and told me to carry things for them. At that point they had already taken Christine. When they asked me, I refused and tried to argue with them. They had women with them who were their maids and their job was to carry everything the men were looting in the village. These women started collecting things and taking them. The men started beating me up using their gun. I fell on the floor, and they kept beating me. My nose was bleeding I was hurting, but they would not stop. Then I heard one of them saying in Kinyarwanda: "Take the girl." They took me. I could hardly walk but they forced me to take their stuff. They tied all of us girls with ropes around our hips so we would not run away. It was so dark that I could not see anybody's face. They told us to start walking. We were going so fast I was out of breath.

At midnight, when we reached the forest, they stopped to look through everything they had stolen in the village. They told us we were going to be their wives. There were thirteen of us girls and some boys. They beat up the boys and left them for dead. They freed three girls after raping them. Then they started fighting to decide who was going to rape me first. I was raped there. I didn't know who did it; I did not see his face. We kept walking through the forest.

When the sun started rising, we saw their faces. We were at their camp. It was like a big village. There were small houses everywhere and a big one in the center.

Their commander came and looked at me and then asked: *"Why didn't you keep this one for me?"*

He asked to know who raped me, and they pointed at a man in the group. He killed that man right there. We were in Ninja. I was held hostage for eight months. I got pregnant from the rape in the commander's compound. One day, the Interahamwes went looting. They called the commander on the radio.

They said; *"We have so many goats and cows, we need more people to come get them."*

He left to go get what his men had looted. He left some of his men to guard us so we did not escape. It was at that moment I realized I had a chance to flee from that place. I sent word to the other girls to get ready; we were going to flee. I was pregnant at the time and since I belonged to the commander, I knew the guards would be nicer to me. I told them I wanted to eat bananas, and I told them to let me go to the market and get some.

Interahamwes have a market where they sell what they loot. They told me I could not leave by myself. They were going to send me with a few men. I asked if Christine could go with me, since she was at camp too. We took containers with us. As we were leaving we heard the alert sound go off - the camp was under attack. Those who went to get the goats were rushing back. Despite that, I knew we had to go on because it was our last chance to escape from hell. The guard told me to go back, and I told him I had to get bananas. He was concerned for his life so he did not insist and let us go.

I held Christine's hand and told her: *"We will die together."*

Gun shots were detonating everywhere. Bombs were exploding and there was a lot of smoke. Christine and I started running; we were going as fast as we could. A bomb exploded close to us and fell on the ground. I could not see Christine anymore. When I looked back, the commander was coming toward me. I could see him in the midst of the smoke. I could not look for Christine anymore. I kept running and the fighting was still raging. I looked back and the commander was not there anymore. Maybe he died when the bombs were exploding from everywhere. I went into the forest, running through the trees.

I did not know where I was going. For eleven days I went like that, not knowing where I was going. I was worried because I was pregnant. I was eating anything I could find. I finally found my way home. People showed me the road and directed me until I got here. I was completely desperate because of what happened to me. I was also sad because I had lost Christine. One day, a lady told me there a woman who was taking care of rape victims. I went to her, and she introduced me to the pastor. I do not have parents. The pastor and his wife took me to their house, and I have been a part of their family. I have given birth to a baby boy. I found Christine here too. I don't have anything and have to beg all the time. I want a new chance in life. I want to be a woman like any other.

Christine

They took me to the bush, and I was a slave for them. Once they went to loot, and they were attacked. We ran away that day. I still have my parents and they welcomed me, but my brothers were mocking me. They were saying I called the Interahamwes to come rape me. I don't know what illness I have, as my belly is swollen. People think I am pregnant but I am not. As for my daughter, people accept her but I can't feed her. I am really worried about the fact that my stomach is hurting. I am traumatized. I have dreams of them raping us in the forest. I sometimes spend a week without eating.

Joice

It happened to me in April 2007. They took me to the forest. I was held in captivity for seven months until the government troops rescued us. There were fifteen girls with me when we arrived at the camp; about ten of them died. Life was really hard there. We were mistreated and threatened all the time. At least two men raped me every day, saying that I was their wife. They were beating us all the time and we could not complain or cry. We were slaves. They did whatever they wanted to us at any time of the day. I am an orphan, for my parents died, though I live with my sister. I wish I could get married. I have never received any medical treatment since I came back from the camp.

Grace

I was fourteen when our village was attacked in 2003. I was at church with some friends. Some of them are here with me. The militiamen circled the church, and we were frightened. People were running as fast as they could without knowing where they were going. In the confusion, my friends and I were slow to leave the place, so we were caught. They circled us, and raped us. They did horrible things to us. They beat us with extreme violence, and tied our hands. I was raped by nine men. It hurt, and my pain would not go away.

Then they took us to their camps. Once we arrived there, they treated us like slaves, raping us all the time. We were nothing more than animals in the eyes of the Interahamwes, we were mere objects. The men did whatever they wanted to us, and always guarded us closely so that we would not run away.

One day, they sent us to the creek to get water for them, and they did not send any men with us. We took courage and fled, running through the bush before we found the road. People helped us and showed us how to get back to our home. I was lucky that my parents accepted me when I came back, because I was pregnant out of wedlock. I later gave birth to a boy, and he is four years old now. Many people mistreat my child because he was born from the Interahamwes.

I am worried because I have neither received appropriate medical treatment nor have I been treated for AIDS. People make fun of me because I am a rape victim. I spent months crying because of what happened to me, and I am ashamed when I meet people because of what has happened to me. I stopped going to school, even though I want to learn and hoped to become a tailor. I wanted to be famous in the village for the good work I have done. I pray that God will send people of good will to come help me.

Berte:

I was kidnapped August 17, 2006. I feel lucky because I was rescued the next day. However, I was raped by a man in Lemera when I was kidnapped. When I was rescued, I was taken to the clinic and tested for AIDS, and luckily my results were negative, which I praise God for. My parents are still alive but they cannot support my schooling.

I would love to have a small business someday to help pay for my schooling, so that I can become a nurse.

Sandra:

May 16, 2007, I was at home when suddenly militiamen came into the house. They tied my dad, looted everything we possessed, and raped me in front of my father. I was fifteen when that happened. I am still in primary school, and my grades are not good because I cannot concentrate. I keep thinking about what happened to me. I don't have any peace in my heart. At school, people laugh at me because they know what happened to me. When you are a victim of sexual violence, everyone mocks you. The village is small and everyone knows what happened to me. My father passed away, so now I am an orphan. Because of that situation I do not know how long I will be able to go to school, even though school is important, and is the only way I can get a chance in life.

Joy:

I was 17 when the Interahamwes kidnapped me. They attacked our village at night. They were searching the house, trying to find money and women. There were two women in my house. They told us to carry the things they had stolen from us. We carried everything, and they led us to the forest. When we arrived in the forest, they raped both of us. There was maybe 20 other girls with us, from different villages. They took us to the forest in Ninja.

When we arrived to their camp, they shared us like a piece of cake. Whoever wanted us would have us, and we would have a different partner each week. Indeed, they raped us all the time. I was there for six months. And I became pregnant while in the camp and gave birth to a boy who does not know who his father is. I gave the child the name Rhushenge which means "Pray to God." One day they sent us to the creek by ourselves because they thought that we would not be able to find our way back home since we arrived at the camp during the night. We decided to take the risk to flee. We knew they would kill us if we failed but we did it anyway.

Two months ago I married a man who does not have a job but loves me just as I am. I had problems with my father, because he keeps sending my mother and I out of the house. He accuses us of calling the Interahamwes to come get me. I do not understand why he would say such things. He was there the day I was abducted. He fled to the plantation and was hiding while they kidnapped me—and he did nothing.

I am expecting a child with my husband; I am praying he will accept the child I had when I was kidnapped. I would love to learn a trade and be useful to society. I want to become a tailor and a designer. I also want to become a counselor for women who went through what I went through.

Faith:

I was 17 when I was raped. It was October 27, 2005. We were home when the Interahamwes came into our house. They shot and killed my father. The Interahamwes came to each house and took all the girls with them, and then we walked for two days. They tied our hands and told us we had to choose a husband. We were afraid and did not say anything, so they chose men for us who became our owners. We stayed there for three months until government troops came to our rescue. I went to the Catholic priests and they took me to Bukavu. I gave birth to a little child, a girl.

My dream is to become a counselor for girls who have been raped, but I also want to have a center to help them economically. It would also be great to design clothes for men and women. That way, I can become independent and prove I am worth something in society. Maybe then a young man will want to marry me. I have, however, forgiven those who have done this to me.

Candice:

I was sleeping when the Interahamwes came to the village. They woke us and took all us girls with them. We went to their camp, and stayed there for five months. They forced us to be with any man that wanted us, and we were beaten in the mornings. I became pregnant and gave birth to a boy; I named him ASIFIWE which means "Praise God."

Later, I married a young man and had a child with him, but he does not like Asifiwe because he was born from a rape.

I hope to become a tailor in the future. I want to make clothes and be able to provide something for my family. Then maybe my husband will stop saying I do not contribute anything to our household.

Alicia:

One night Interahamwes came to our village. They took me and five other girls. While I was in their village, I became anemic. I succeeded in fleeing from their camp after being there five months. I returned to my parents and gave birth to a boy I called Chance. But my parents divorced because of this child. I have now met someone, and we are planning to get married.

Nadine:

We went to school in the morning. I was 16 at the time. We did not know that Interahamwes were hiding behind our school. When the director of the school found out that Interahamwes were around the school, he fled and all of the students panicked. Everyone ran as fast as they could without knowing where they were going. No one knew where to go. In the rush, an Interahamwe kidnapped me.

They took us to their camp in the middle of the forest. Then they formed a circle and placed us in the middle, asking me if I wanted to choose one of them as my husband. But I did not say anything, so they tied us to a tree for three days. We did not have any food or water during this time. They came back on the third day and shot two other girls. They asked me if I still did not want to have sex with one of them. They threatened me and told me that if I refused, they would kill two others. They forced me to look at the bleeding corpses of the two other girls, so I ended up accepting. All of them raped me. I was taken to their camp until the day the national army rescued us. Now I have a child who will never know who his real father is.

I want to become a tailor and be able to make money so that I can feed my child. Maybe there will be a man willing to take me as I am. We need prayers because people hate us. They say that we are a curse to the community. But we did not ask to be raped. Maybe if we became active members of the society by being useful economically we would gain more respect.

APPENDIX C:

A LITTLE HISTORY

The Democratic republic of Congo is located in central Africa. It is 905,063 square miles and is home to about sixty million people. The capital of the Democratic Republic of Congo is Kinshasa; it has a population of about eight million people. It is the third largest country in the continent and home to the Congo River. Congo started as a private property of King Leopold the Second. King Leopold called it the Free State of Congo. The book "King Leopold Ghost" talks about massive atrocities conducted at that time. It gives an estimate of a million people dying as a result of these atrocities.

In 1907, the country was handed over to the Belgian government to become the Belgian Congo. After a series of riots, the Belgian government granted independence to the country on June 30, 1960. Patrice Emery Lumumba was the first prime minister and Joseph Kasavubu was elected president. The country was then reamed Democratic Republic of Congo. The years following the independence of the country were marked by violence and instability. There was an army mutiny and the rich southern province of Katanga attempted to become independent. The prime minister, Patrice Emery Lumumba died in the midst of these events. His death led to rebellions that lasted until 1965 when Mobutu took the power claiming that he would only keep it for five years.

Mobutu quickly took over the power and kept it without sharing. He re-named the country Zaïre and required citizens to abandon their European names and take African names only. Mobutu had to face rebellion in Katanga in 1977 and 1978, but the rebels were driven out with the help of Belgian troops. He instated a one-party rule in the country with all the powers centralized around him. With the end of the cold war, pressures started increasing on Mobutu to open up the political arena in Zaïre. In 1990 he finally agreed to allow a multiple party system and elections. Things kept getting worse. In 1991, unpaid soldiers looted Kinshasa, the capital of the country, to protest because they did not receive their wages. This event destroyed more of the country's economy that was already faltering since the late eighties.

In 1994, a million Rwandan refugees fled to Zaïre and settled in refugee camps in the eastern region. Meanwhile political unrest in Kinshasa was weakening the country. In 1996, the conflict in Rwanda spilled into Zaire. The Tutsi-led Rwandan government sent troops in Zaïre to support an armed coalition led by Laurent Desire Kabila. The coalition was named Alliance des Forces Démocratiques pour la Libération du Congo-Zaïre (AFDL). AFDL, with the support of Rwandan and Ugandan troops, marched toward Kinshasa to overthrow Mobutu. Failed peace talks between Kabila and Mobutu resulted to the fall of Kinshasa in 1997. Kabila became the third president of Zaïre on May 17, 1997. Mobutu fled to Morocco where he died.

Kabila renamed the country Democratic Republic of Congo. He concentrated power around the AFDL, but the army was in the hands of Rwandans. The next year, relationships started deteriorating between Kabila and his foreign allies. He ordered Rwandan troops to leave the territory of the Democratic Republic of Congo. Rwandan troops refused to leave the country. August 2, 1998, fighting erupted all over the country between Rwandan and Congolese troops. Two days later Rwandan troops flew to Bas Congo, the western province of DR Congo, with the intent of taking

Kinshasa. Their goal was to replace Kabila with the new rebel group, the Rassemblement Congolais pour la Démocratie (RCD). Their plans failed when Angola, Namibia and Zimbabwe sent troops to rescue the government of Kabila. Rwandan troops and RCD took control of the eastern part of the country and continued fighting Kabila and his new allies.

In 1999 a new rebellion started in northern Congo. Ugandan troops allied themselves with ex-Mobutu supporters to create "The Mouvement pour la Liberation du Congo" (MLC). They took over the northern part of the country. At that point the country was divided into 3 parts: the government, the RCD and MLC.

In January 2001, Kabila was assassinated by his bodyguard in the presidential palace. His son Joseph replaced him and was more open to negotiations and willing to cooperate with the international community. He allowed the deployment of UN forces, and sought dialogue both with the Congolese rebels and with foreign governments. He was able to negotiate a peaceful departure of all foreign troops from Congolese soil.

In October 2001, a process started in Addis Ababa, Ethiopia led to the Inter-Congolese dialogue in Sun City, South Africa in February 2002. The dialogue resulted in the formation of a transitional government that included all rebel forces and political parties. Each main rebel force was given a vice president position.

In December 2005, Congolese people voted for a new constitution that became effective on February 18, 2006.

June 30, 2006, Congolese people voted for the first time in a free election since their independence. 25 million people registered to elect a president among the 33 candidates and 500 representatives among the 9,500 candidates. Joseph Kabila won the first round with 44% of the votes but had to throw a runoff against his vice president Jean Pierre Bemba. Clashes and instability marked the election period but the election itself was judged fair by international observers. Kabila won the runoff and became the first elected president of the Democratic Republic of Congo. He was elected for a five year term.

The country is still struggling to bring peace back in the east. In 2008, clashes involving the government troops and militias particularly the one led by Laurent Nkunda had caused hundreds of thousands of people to flee their homes. An effort is being made to bring back peace to the eastern Congo, but the road to peace is still long. Relationships with the country's eastern neighbor have improved. The hope is that we will soon see better days for the people of the Democratic Republic of Congo. Meanwhile abuse, use of child soldiers, and rape are still common in mountains of Eastern Congo.

The Democratic Republic of Congo is at a turning point in its history. The country is struggling to restore peace and start a reconstruction process. The government has made very little progress in accomplishing these goals. The eastern part of the country is still under the threat of foreign and local militias who have ruled these regions for years. Even though they have lost their strength, they are still a threat to the peace of the region. Two major militias have remained in eastern Congo: CNDP and FDLR. They have proven themselves to be a threat to the people and to the fragile peace in Eastern Congo. They fight each other and the government. They have also been deeply involved in illegal exploitation and exportation of mineral. That is how they have funded their weapons. They committed gross human rights violations (including indiscriminate killings, rapes, and forced child soldier recruitment) in the areas under their control.

In January 2008, the government of the Democratic Republic of Congo and 20 militia groups signed an agreement for disengagement of rebel forces and their integration to the national army. All parties respected the cease fire agreement under the monitoring of the UN except for the CNDP of Laurent Nkunda. In August 2008, heavy fighting broke out between the national army and CNDP troops. The fighting led to another humanitarian catastrophe.

A quarter million people were displaced. Hundreds of people were killed over four months of conflicts. CNDP troops, more organized and better disciplined, defeated the national army. They proclaimed a unilateral cease fire at the gate of Goma, the capital of the province. The international community worked an agreement between the two parties in order to keep the fighting out of the city. During this period, the United States, European Union, and United Nations all worked to develop plans for a lasting peace and seek adherence to past agreements, but the progress was slow.

January 2009 saw a dramatic change in both the political and military realm in Nord Kivu. Leadership conflict between Nkunda and his chief of staff led to a partition of the rebel group. The main faction led by Bosco Ntaganda signed an agreement with the government and integrated the national army. Pareco, another main militia also did the same. The governments of the D.R.Congo and Rwanda, which had been engaged in the gradual pursuit of rapprochement over several months, announced plans for Rwandan forces to enter the D.R.C. and join with the Congolese military in a concerted effort to eliminate the FDLR once and for all.

On January 20, 2009, several thousand Rwandan soldiers crossed into the D.R.Congo for the third time in twelve years, but this time at the invitation of the Congolese Government in Kinshasa. Two days later, Laurent Nkunda fled into Rwanda, where Rwandan officials took him into custody. He remains in custody as of August 2009, pending the resolution of Rwandan court proceedings. Between January 20 and the end of February 2009, the joint Rwandan-Congolese-CNDP-PARECO coalition of forces pressured the FDLR, engaged in a small number of battles with FDLR units, and convinced several hundred FDLR members and their families to return voluntarily to Rwanda. On February 25, 2009, the Rwandan forces left the D.R.C.

The Congolese government signed agreements with rebel forces in March 2009. Rebel forces registered as political parties and their troops were integrated into the national army. The national army, with the help of the UN, has launched an operation against the FDLR in North and South Kivu. These operations have the objective of freeing Eastern Congo from the FDLR. Unfortunately, human rights violations by the FDLR and by undisciplined FARDC elements have increased since Kimia II began.

The northeast of the country has also experienced great unrest recently. The Congolese army (FARDC) has engaged the Lord's

Resistance Army (LRA). The LRA is led by the infamous Joseph Kony and has been involved in brutal human rights violations in the Ituri including rape, torture, looting and other exactions against the local population.LRA also conducted abductions of children to make the boys child soldiers and the girls sex slaves. On December 15, 2008, the governments of Uganda, the D.R.C. and southern Sudan launched a joint military operation, Operation Lightning Thunder, to capture or kill senior LRA commanders. The operation was launched after it became clear to regional governments that Kony was not interested in signing an UN-negotiated peace agreement. The D.R.C. Government authorized troops from the Ugandan People's Defense Force (UPDF) to enter the D.R.Congo. The operation officially ended in March 2009 when the majority of UPDF troops withdrew from the D.R.C. The Congolese army launched another operation against the LRA but the rebel movement is still committing crimes and Joseph Kony is still roaming free.

It is in the context at the crossroad of history that the Democratic Republic of Congo is struggling to find its way to peace and reconstruction. The challenges that face the leaders of the country are great after 32 years of dictatorship and more than ten years of war. The crisis in Eastern Congo remains the main challenge for the country.

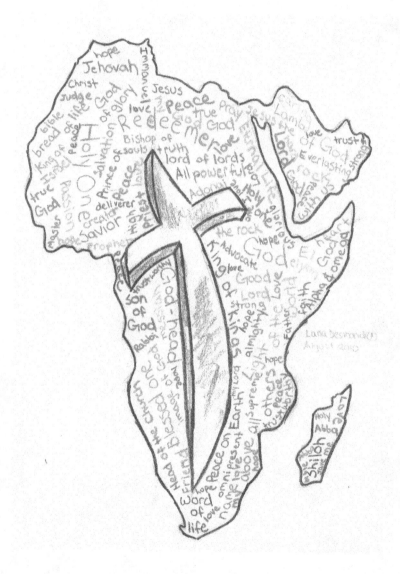

GLOSSARY OF TERMS

AFDL: Alliance of Democratic Forces for the Liberation of Congo played a key part in ending the Mobutu dictatorship, and putting Kabila in power

Bideka: Rural village in Sud Kivu province located 41 km from Bukavu

Bukavu: Capital of Sud Kivu, with approximately 250,000

DMF: Dikembe Mutombo Foundation

FARDC: Armed Forces of the Democratic Republic of Congo, state military organization set up to defend the DRC

FDLR: Democratic Forces for the Liberation of Rwanda, a Hutu rebel group operating primarily out of the eastern DRC

Goma: Capital city of the Nord-Kivu province

Interahamwe: Hutu paramilitary organization

Jean Pierre Bemba: Leader of the MLC, He is being tried for war crimes at ICJ

Joseph Kabila: Current president of the DRC

Joseph Kasavubu: First President of the DRC

Jules Mutebutsi: War Lord in Sud Kivu

Kadogo: Term used for child soldiers in The DRC Congo

Katanga: Southern province in the DRC

Kidodobo: Rural town in Sud Kivu

King Leopold II: Belgian founder and sole owner of the Congo Free State, which includes the DRC

Kinkole: A rural zone east of Kinshasa

Kinshasa: Capital and largest city of the DRC, currently over 10 million residents

Kinyarwanda: Language spoken in Rwanda

Laurent Nkunda: Former war lord operating in Sud Kivu

Laurent-Désiré Kabila: President of the DRC from '97 to '01, when assassinated

MLC: Movement for the Liberation of Congo, a rebel group in the northern DRC, assisted by the Ugandan government

Mobutu Sese seko: Second President of DR Congo

Mudaka: Rural town 8.6 km SE from Bukavu

Mumosho: Rural village of Sud Kivu

Mundundu 40: Paramilitary militia operating in eastern Congo

PARECO: Military group allied with the FDLR

Patrice Emery Lumumba: African anti-colonial leader, first legally elected Prime Minister of the Congo, later assassinated

PTSD: Post traumatic Stress Disorder

RCD: Rally for Congolese Democracy, a rebel group in the eastern DRC, assisted by the Rwandan government

Sud Kivu: A province of the eastern DRC, its capital, Bukavu

UPDF: Uganda People's Defense Force, formerly the National Resistance Army, Uganda's armed forces

Zaïre: Former name of the DRC, from 1971 to 1997; also known as the Belgian Congo until 1960

Vision of Mwangaza International in the Democratic Republic of Congo

In recent years we have distributed clothing and basic hygienic supplies to women and children affected by the wars in Congo. We have also begun leading seminars with village leaders on how to counsel rape victims in their communities. These little things are the first steps in our vision to bring healing to the country and to others like it.

In the future, we hope to expand our training program so that village leaders can learn how to adequately take care of their own people.

Our primary goal is to establish what we call healing centers. These centers are properties where women and children are taken in and put into families - not into a system. Those still young enough attend school and funds are established to make post-secondary studies available. Adults are encouraged to learn a trade that they can use to reestablish themselves in the society.

All who take part in the healing centers are given physical and psychological treatment through clinics and spiritual counseling.

The value of this holistic approach for Congo will be seen when it no longer has millions displaced and struggling to stay alive, but instead has lost generations working together to rebuild the society.

Even before that, though, the value of the healing centers will be seen when one orphan hears the word "love" where he once heard "kill." It will be seen when one abandoned woman receives a new family that will never abandon her.

This is our vision. This is what will happen when we partner together.

Visit our website for more information:
www.mwangazaint.com
Our Goal is to establish:

1. A shelter for victims of sexual violence in Bideka
2. A shelter for victims of human trafficking in Kinshasa
3. A school in Kinshasa
4. A medical clinic in Lodja

We also want to establish a scholarship fund to help war victims get an education and we want to set up small business loans for women.

Contact us if you want to read our proposals for these projects:
mwangazaint@gmail.com

CPSIA information can be obtained
at www.ICGtesting.com
Printed in the USA
BVHW070727030821
613416BV00001B/13